Managed Care and Capitation:

ISSUES IN NURSING

By Teri Britt, MS, RN, Cheryl Schraeder, PhD, RN, and Paul Shelton, EdD

AMERICAN NURSES ASSOCIATION

Library of Congress Cataloging-in-Publication Data

Britt, Teri.
    Managed care and capitation : issues in nursing practice / Teri
Britt, Cheryl Schraeder, Paul Shelton.
       p.   cm.
    ISBN 1-55810-141-1 (paper)
    1. Nursing—Effect of managed care on.   2. Managed care programs
(Medical care) I. Schraeder, Cheryl. II. Shelton, Paul.
III. Title.
    [DNLM: 1. Managed Care Programs—economics nurses' instruction.
2. Capitation Fee nurses' instruction.   W 130.1 B862m 1998]
RT82.B75   1998
610.73—dc21
DNLM/DLC
for Library of Congress   98-3607
                                                       CIP

Published by American Nurses Publishing
600 Maryland Avenue, SW
Suite 100 West
Washington, DC 20024-2571

9803MC   1M   10/98

About the Authors

Teri Britt, MS, RN, is a research analyst at the Health Systems Research Center of Carle Clinic Association. She has participated in numerous studies exploring and evaluating health care delivery models for the frail and elderly, and her work has been published in nursing and health care journals and texts. A doctoral candidate in health policy and administration at The Pennsylvania State University, Ms. Britt has clinical experience in geriatric and community nursing, nursing case management, and capitated systems.

Cheryl Schraeder, PhD, RN, heads the Health Systems Research Center of Carle Clinic Association. She is experienced in nursing case management models, health services research, and development of health delivery models for the elderly, and she is an adjunct faculty member at the University of Illinois College of Medicine.

Paul Shelton, EdD, is a research analyst at the Health Systems Research Center of Carle Clinic Association. He has more than 20 years of experience in the health care field, including health services research, management training and development, and various human resource activities.

Acknowledgments

Appreciation is expressed to the reviewers who provided guidance in the preparation of this monograph:

Virginia Burggraf, DNS, RN, C, American Nurses Foundation
Christine de Vries, American Nurses Association
Gerri Lamb, PhD, RN, FAAN, Carondelet Health Network
Kathleen Overton, RN, NMCC, BlueCross, BlueShield of the
    National Capital Area

Contents

Introduction

Managed care systems have proliferated at an unprecedented pace in the past two decades. The effects of this growth are quite complex and have had controversial and far-reaching repercussions for nursing. The transition from fee-for-service health care to managed care has changed the way care is delivered, organized, and financed. These changes have triggered serious debate. Some view managed care as an opportunity to control growth in spending, whereas others see managed care as a threat to health care quality.

Managed care, whether in the form of public, private, or not-for-profit, is now the dominant type of health coverage in the United States. Public opinion on managed care is filled with inconsistencies. For instance, consumers generally report high rates of satisfaction with managed care plans, yet most consumers favor government regulation of managed care even if it increases cost (Blendon et al. 1998). Blendon et al. point out that public opinion polls indicate that a majority of individuals perceive that managed care has hurt the quality of care available and is not doing as good a job for patients as other professions and institutions in health care (such as hospitals, nurses, and physicians). In addition, there is general concern that patients may not receive the care they need when they are very sick. The fact remains, however, that most people with managed care coverage give it high satisfaction ratings (Blendon et al. 1998).

Consumers and policymakers have reacted strongly to the controversies within managed care, as evidenced by the introduction in both the Congress and state legislatures of more than 1,000 bills on consumer protection under managed care (Blendon et al. 1998). From a health professional's perspective, managed care certainly has had a major impact on career opportunities, roles, and financial compensation for nursing care. The complex issues surrounding managed care are far beyond the scope of this monograph. Instead, the information offered here is intended to outline several of the basic principles of managed care and some of the associated implications for nursing. The reader is encouraged to think critically about the information provided and determine how the basic, sometimes theoretical, concepts of managed care are operationalized in the clinical setting.

Many have questioned whether there actually are roles for nurses in managed care environments. The authors of this monograph take the stand that opportunities exist for nursing and that managed care systems can benefit from nursing involvement at all levels. Other authors have voiced a similar perspective (Christianson, Taylor, and Knutson 1998; Lamb, Donaldson, and Kellogg 1997; Lamb 1995; Parr 1996; Rustia and Bartek 1997; Daly 1997; Scheffler, Waitzman, and Hillman 1996; Simpson 1997). This somewhat optimistic position is tempered by the notion that creativity, innovation, and dogged persistence will be required in order for nurses to seek, identify, and develop roles in the changing health care environment.

Historically, nurses have generally had limited participation in the financing and structuring of care. Although there are notable exceptions to this statement (as evidenced by the number of nurse executives and journals focusing on administrative nursing), most nurses do not have education or experience in health economics, finance, or business management. These functions have been performed by physicians, hospitals, insurance companies, and state and federal governments (e.g., Medicare and Medicaid). Traditionally, the discipline of nursing has focused primarily on patient care. Caring for the patient was the overriding theme of clinical practice, education, and research in nursing. Generally, this emphasis provided a thorough base of clinical knowledge, but left nurses minimally prepared in financial or business expertise. This practice is changing.

Today's challenge is to maintain the theme of high quality patient care at the forefront of nursing, while simultaneously transitioning to more active involvement in the financial aspects of care delivery. A balanced approach to care that encompasses the totality of the person has long been the goal of nursing. However, cost consciousness in the face of limited health care dollars has reached a level that crosses all care settings and patient populations to a much greater extent than in the past. It has created a heightened awareness of the need to provide cost-effective care in a clinically responsible manner. Additionally, documentation drawing correlations between nursing care and patient outcomes (financial as well as clinical) is a very real challenge faced by most nurse managers, administrators, educators, and researchers. These goals are not always easy to reconcile. This situation requires that nurses be informed, active participants and advocates in the health care system.

Nursing has two choices: Ignore the importance of financing structures or become actively informed and involved in shaping delivery structures. Although learning about managed care and capitation is arduous and perhaps never-ending work, the benefits far outweigh the costs. For instance, managed care organizations (MCOs) with capitated payment mechanisms could potentially provide nurses stronger forums for patient education, advocacy, and preventive efforts across care settings. The ethical questions arising from managed care and a capitated financing environment will benefit from an informed and active voice representing the nursing perspective. If the discipline of nursing is to continue to play an integral part in health care delivery, nurses must seize this opportunity to shape their collective future by establishing a proactive and educated stance.

Perhaps one of the biggest barriers health care providers face in understanding managed care and capitation is the transition from concentrating on an individual patient to focusing more on patient aggregates or specific populations. This broader picture cannot be well understood without a thorough knowledge of individualized patient care; nursing has this strong knowledge base coupled with a fine tradition of community-based care. In many ways, the emergence of managed care and capitation represent critical opportunities for nursing to influence the future of health care delivery and financing. Nurses must be poised to face this challenge by acquiring and using accurate information, responsible strategies, and a strong clinical foundation. These skills will be necessary in order to sort through the complexities of managed care and its implications for patients as well as for the nursing profession.

The relationships between the delivery and financing of care are perhaps now more complex and intertwined than ever before in health care. MCOs often administer both the delivery and financing aspects of health care, so it is important to understand the various incentives of insurers, employer groups, health care providers, and consumers. This monograph introduces the basic concepts of managed care, focusing on the implications for nursing.

Basic concepts central to capitated health care delivery and financing, such as population-based care strategies, risk models, utilization management, information management, and measurement of quality outcomes, are examined herein. The basic concepts may be operationalized quite differently in various managed care settings. A case study is included that describes a nurse-lead delivery model for capitated care for Medicare beneficiaries. Although multiple sources are available on each of these concepts, the intent is to portray each within a nursing perspective. The end of each chapter contains a section devoted to implications for the nursing profession.

The monograph is organized to focus first on introducing the principal ideas behind managed care delivery structures, making note of how the structures are tied to financial systems. Then these basic notions are intertwined with the concepts of population-based care and risk sharing. The sections on outcomes management and information systems point to future areas for intense nursing involvement and potential career opportunities. The relationships between all of these concepts are complex; it is hoped that presenting the material layer by layer will enable readers to formulate ideas about how the changes in health care may affect their career paths and how nursing input is needed to improve the health care system.

Understanding the central concepts presented here is a step toward meeting larger goals. Although health care is changing rapidly, the vision of nursing is stable. This vision, which can carry us into the next century, is still based on fostering stronger systems to support patient care, facilitating the growth of knowledge to make maximum use of resources, and establishing and maintaining delivery structures that promote patient health, well-being, and satisfaction.

2

Capitation Within a Managed Care Context

CHAPTER OBJECTIVES

- Describe major forces emerging from managed care.
- Explain how capitated financing fits within managed care.
- Highlight implications for nursing.

Managed care presents the discipline of nursing with complex challenges. For example, the move toward managed care had been accompanied by staff reductions in many areas. Some critics have pointed out the dangers in limited access to specialty and emergency care. These areas have been the focus of heated debate in the popular and professional literature. Much of the controversy centers on the dynamic relationships between the delivery and financing of care that have consequences for patients and health care providers.

Many nurses have experienced shifts in role functions or career opportunities as a result of managed care. Nursing needs to provide expertise within a managed care context. For instance, nurses are well-equipped with clinical knowledge to help assess patients' needs, triage patients into appropriate levels of care, and evaluate the quality of care provided. More generally, nurses will play a critical role in examining and implementing ways to improve the health care system to make it more optimal.

Nurses must be informed about managed care and about the implications of this delivery and financing structure, which has an impact on patients as well as the discipline of nursing. This chapter presents an overview of trends evolving as a result of the transition to managed care. It covers basic principles related to organizational forms and financing approaches, but does not explore more complex descriptions of how the principles play out in the diverse world of practice. Readers are encouraged to apply these concepts to the unique practice situations they encounter. Selected implications for the discipline of nursing are given.

Major Forces Emerging from Managed Care

Managed care has changed the way health care services are accessed, provided, and paid for. In the traditional system, fee-for-service financing placed incentives on providers to order and deliver services. The more services that were provided, the greater the financial benefit to the provider. From the patient's perspective, more services also were seen as better, even though some services may have been requested that were clinically unnecessary. This practice further encouraged the use of services, particularly since most services were covered by a third party and were not paid out of pocket by patients.

Managed care reverses these incentives for patients, plans, and providers. For example, patients are encouraged (by no or low co-payments) to access preventive and primary care instead of specialty services. Health plans are encouraged to contract with cost-effective providers. Providers have incentives to increase productivity. Instead of encouraging service use, the incentive is to keep individuals (and populations) healthy so that the demand for health care services is managed in a predictable and cost-efficient manner. When individuals become sick, the plan and provider usually have incentives to provide cost-effective, efficiently targeted services without excess or duplication. Incentives overlap, conflict, and change. As a result of managed care, the issue has switched from concern about overutilization to concern about underutilization.

In addition to changing incentives for providers, managed care has drastically changed the relationship between insurers and enrollees of health plans. In traditional indemnity plans, the financial risk was held by the insurer. The enrollee paid relatively large deductibles and premiums and, when health services were used, filed claims. In managed care, the risk is more evenly distributed between the insurer and insured enrollee. Enrollees are responsible for co-payments and monthly payroll deductions in varying combinations according to individual plan specifications. In general, the enrollee pays a portion of each rendered service, which must be authorized by the primary care provider. This practice differs from indemnity insurance, where once the deductible and premiums were met, the enrollee did not have to pay a significant portion for care rendered and this care could be accessed from any provider the patient chose.

Trends Supporting Managed Care

The 1980s witnessed a major change in health care cost-containment strategies. These trends have affected the way managed care has evolved in the current decade. Four important aspects of these changes have been identified (Thorpe 1995):

- Private payers and employer groups increased efforts to institute cost containment.
- State governments and Medicare investigated innovative approaches to hospital rate setting [e.g., diagnosis related groups (DRGs)].
- Public and private sectors encouraged hospitals to compete on price rather than other parameters.
- Cost-containment efforts also reached beyond health care institutions to focus on physician/provider payment.

In response to these and other factors, the health maintenance organization (HMO) approach to care became quite prominent. In fact, managed care has become the dominant form of health insurance in the United States. Early research comparing managed care to fee-for-service care indicated that managed care approaches reduced overall health expenditures (Prospective Payment Assessment Commission 1997). However, questions arose about whether the results could really be attributed to managed care financing and delivery systems or if they were due to other factors. For instance, factors that may have contributed to expenditure reduction included differing practice patterns of physicians in HMOs versus traditional health plans, differences in enrollment patterns (healthier people tended to enroll in managed care plans), and HMO marketing strategies that favored healthier persons (Thorpe 1995, Luft 1981).

Changing Incentives

As noted previously, managed care changes the way patients, providers, and payers are rewarded. The patient is encouraged (by minimal or no co-payments) to access preventive and health maintenance care through a primary care provider (PCP). In most cases, this person (usually a primary care physician or nurse practitioner) acts as the entry point and gatekeeper for services. The provider (PCP, clinic, hospital) is contracted to provide care to a population for a set payment. This payment arrangement creates an incentive to provide cost-effective care. Ideally, the result is high quality preventive and primary care services with selective referral to specialists, hospitals, and other service providers. However, it may also mean pressure on providers to be productive in terms of high patient volumes. The MCO or payer is encouraged to recruit healthy individuals or groups that will not cost as much to cover. In addition, plans tend to contract with providers that have a cost-effective track record. Employer groups, however, have the choice of which managed care product(s) to offer to particular groups of employees, and most employer groups consist of both healthy and at-risk populations. Employer groups generally decide on the basis of the mix of employees whether to choose an HMO, HMO with preferred provider organization (PPO), or HMO with PPO and indemnity to offer their employees. From this discussion, it becomes apparent that the relationships and incentives among providers, employer groups, and health plans are quite complex.

Organizational Forms

MCOs vary according to the way they are structured, staffed, and financed [e.g., PPOs, point of service (POS), independent practice association (IPA), etc.]. These models have been described elsewhere (May, Schraeder, and Britt 1997). The intent of this chapter is to provide an overview of managed care and capitated structures rather than to define the various types of MCOs. Classic features of HMOs include the following (Luft 1981):

- Serving a defined population of voluntarily enrolled individuals;
- Accepting the responsibility and financial risk of providing services as contracted by the plan; and
- Receiving a fixed annual or monthly payment from enrollees independent of the actual use of services.

As MCOs have evolved, they have taken on various organizational forms. At one end of the continuum are MCOs that are structured as insurance companies and contract with physicians to provide a specified range of services to groups of individual enrollees. This type of organization typically tries to influence provider behavior by using financial incentives and penalties tied to care utilization and productivity (measured in patients seen per unit of time). Practitioner involvement in

management decisions is minimal in this type of arrangement (Wagner 1996).

At the opposite end of the continuum are well-established, group/staff model HMOs. Traditional MCOs are generally non-profit, integrated delivery systems that employ their own staff of providers. Care is primarily provided in facilities owned by the MCO. The physicians and other staff are typically involved in decision making and planning regarding their practices and their patients (Wagner 1996). Most MCOs fall somewhere in between these two extreme ends of the spectrum. The most popular forms currently are HMO, HMO with PPO option, and HMO with PPO and indemnity.

Whether managed care plans can reduce expenditures in the long term remains to be seen. However, managed care entities, particularly HMOs, have structural and organizational components that, if used optimally, could result in more comprehensive, accessible, and coordinated care (Wagner 1996). These components hold promising opportunities for nursing.

Characteristics of Traditional HMOs

Traditional MCOs share many characteristics that can be optimized to provide high quality patient care. These have been identified as (Wagner 1996)

- Clearly defined population;
- Enrollees who are linked with a primary care provider;
- Integrated services, providers, facilities;
- Integrated financial and clinical data systems;
- Balance of professional power between primary and specialty care providers;
- Unifying mission, culture, and organizational identity among providers;
- Centralized resources such as patient education and home care; and
- Preventive orientation.

These features provide the potential to manage the care of patient populations more effectively. For instance, they make it possible to identify patients with specific health problems, monitor health status, and track service use longitudinally. If used to their maximum potential, these characteristics can support health care providers in optimizing outcomes and managing costs by facilitating effective service delivery without duplications or gaps in care. To make the structural characteristics work effectively, however, organizational arrangements and leadership must support population-based management with resources and staff capable of systematic care delivery (Wagner 1996).

Nursing roles in managed care are linked to these structures. Nurses can optimize the care opportunities available within managed care environments in many ways. For instance, offering health screening and education for enrollee groups, monitoring health promotion practices (e.g., mammography rates), providing case management, coordinating home care, and analyzing outcomes data all hold potential for nursing involvement and leadership. Although opportunities in hospital nursing are becoming more limited, nursing roles in primary care are expanding. The increased number of nurse practitioners in primary care is expected to continue (Mundinger 1994).

Capitated Financing Within a Managed Care Context

As noted in the previous section, managed care can assume a variety of organizational forms. Capitation is the financing structure that characterizes most MCOs. Even within a traditional health care delivery system, some of the patients who access care will be covered under capitated financing structures, so it is important for nurses to be aware of the role of capitated financing in managed care.

It has been suggested that the transformation from fee for service to capitation has been the most significant change in financing care in the United States since the adoption of Medicare's prospective payment system in 1983 (Grimaldi 1995). One of the most obvious changes capitation brings is the shift in financial risk from the payers to insurers and providers. This shift has brought many new ideas and terms to an already complex language of health care.

Managed care has a vocabulary all its own. In this new era of health care, a few definitions must

be shared so that terms can be clearly understood by all the stakeholders. The following section provides an overview of selected terms with basic explanations. These basic concepts will then be used to identify and describe the implications of risk sharing that accompany managed care.

Capitation: The Financial Specifics

Capitation is the per capita payment an MCO receives to provide or arrange a defined package of health services for its members. The services may be provided by the MCO itself, or through contractual arrangements with other providers. The individual member is responsible for following the MCO's administrative policies regarding covered services. Capitation payments cover a fixed period of time and are usually adjusted on the basis of actuarial factors such as age and gender. Unlike fee for service, capitation payments do not vary on the basis of services provided (Grimaldi 1995).

Per Member Per Month

Capitation payments are expressed in terms of per member per month (PMPM). The MCO receives the specified rate for each month each member is enrolled. In very simple terms, the capitation rate can be calculated by dividing the MCO's projected total costs by the total number of member months (Grimaldi 1995).

For the MCO to budget accordingly, the MCO divides total costs into several broad categories such as health expenses and overhead. Health expenses can be further subdivided into categories of service use such as emergency room care, hospital days, and physician office visits (Grimaldi 1995).

Likewise, overhead can be subdivided into member months. Fixed overhead costs are those that do not vary with enrollment size. The greater proportion of fixed overhead costs, the greater the need for the MCO to maintain a specific market share to survive financially. If the MCO's market share decreases markedly, the PMPM fixed cost would rise, potentially making the MCO less able to compete with other MCOs in the marketplace (Grimaldi 1995).

Different Capitation Rating Systems

Two types of rating systems are widely used to calculate capitation rates: community and experience rates. Community rating systems distribute the risk and cost of health services equally among all plan members. MCOs using this type of rating system charge the same rate to all enrollees regardless of health status or projected utilization rates. In community rating systems, healthier members essentially subsidize those who use more services. If this subsidy causes enrollee payments to be too high, healthy enrollees have a strong incentive to shop for plans that offer an experience-based capitation rate (Grimaldi 1995).

Experience-based capitation rates are based on utilization patterns and cost histories of enrollees or groups. Under this system, MCOs charge different groups different rates. Experience rating means that groups that have historically consumed more services pay higher capitation rates. Factors that contribute to the calculation of experience-based rates include age, gender, health status, and occupation (Grimaldi 1995).

Full Capitation Versus Partial Capitation

MCOs may be fully or partially capitated. Fully capitated MCOs are financially liable for providing all the services in the benefit package. Partially capitated MCOs are financially liable only for the expenses incurred in rendering the particular services covered by the partial rate. Typically these services are acute hospital inpatient stays, outpatient prescriptions, or anesthesiology (Grimaldi 1995).

Some MCOs provide primary care services under capitation. Usually these MCOs also are required to coordinate specialty care and referrals under the plan. Acceptance of capitation rates also has become a way for specialists and subspecialists to bolster their marketing and negotiating efforts (Grimaldi 1995).

Summary

The previous sections have briefly described the historical and social factors contributing to the expansion of managed care. They have introduced basic concepts related to the incentives of stakeholders and elements of capitated financing. In summary, managed care presents challenges as well as potentials. The structural components of MCOs (e.g., a stable, enrolled population, each member linked with a primary care provider, linked clinical and financial information systems) hold great possibilities that have yet to be fully realized. Nurses must be well acquainted with financial concepts in order to position the discipline proactively for future developments.

Implications for Nursing

The movement toward capitation, the shifts in risk, and the financial implications of health service utilization raise many questions pertaining to the allocation of health resources. Nurses in all settings have been or will be affected by these changes and the issues surrounding them. Proactively shaping patient care now requires new ideas and strategies.

Many of the skills that are required of nurses in managed care are the same ones nurses have always used with patients; however, the skills may be manifested a bit differently. For instance, nurses must rely on critical thinking to respond to these changes in the delivery of health care. Critical thinking includes thinking in diverse ways, seeing things from varying perspectives, and imagining many possible solutions to issues. The application of critical analysis will be essential to rethinking nursing practice, research, and education (Miller and Babcock 1996). These skills will be essential as nurses re-conceptualize their role in health care planning, delivery, and evaluation.

Changes within health care financing structures will continue to affect the discipline of nursing. Nursing roles are moving from an emphasis on the acute setting toward that of ambulatory care and the community. Nursing involvement is also required in the care of persons with chronic illness and those needing long-term care. Many of these roles include caring for populations as well as individuals (Clouten and Weber 1994).

Today's health care involves not only clinical care but also heavy emphasis on financial components. Applying sound clinical principles, understanding the relationships between stakeholders, and identifying the incentives various parties hold in health care places the nurse in an excellent position to advocate for patients. In most reputable MCOs, coverage and delivery decisions are based on clinical need and not solely on considerations of cost. However, nurses may have occasion to facilitate this process when service is denied. For instance, if an MCO denies a service to a patient on the basis of a disagreement regarding the value of an intervention compared with its short-term cost, the nurse may identify and communicate the long-run cost savings potential of the intervention. The nurse can then assist the patient in appealing to the MCO in clinical and financial terms that will meet the MCO's need for cost containment as well as the patient's clinical need. Usually, up to three levels of appeal are available to patients who believe they have been inappropriately denied coverage. Alternatively, nurses may help patients understand the clinical rationale for limited or denied coverage when the requested service is not clinically indicated.

In managed care the focus is not just on individual patients. Nurses have a long tradition of demonstrated competency in caring for groups of patients. New nursing roles will require a comprehensive set of clinical skills coupled with a willingness to explore new population-based strategies. In addition, sharing skills in population-based care with other health care professionals (such as physicians) may enable health care systems to deliver more optimal patient care.

Nurses also may find themselves negotiating on their own behalf in financial arenas. For instance, salary justification statements may be made based on cost savings projections tied to care coordination, case management, and preventive services. Knowledge of health care financing mechanisms and terminology places the nurse in a better position to articulate how nursing skills can make a positive impact on clinical and financial outcomes.

3

Health Care Financing: Definitions and Background

CHAPTER OBJECTIVES

- Examine factors leading to changes in the way health care is delivered and financed.
- Discuss the traditional fee-for-service method of payment.
- Outline trends supporting the transition from fee-for-service to prospective payment.
- Examine the major components of capitated financing systems.
- Discuss trends in integrated delivery systems.
- Discuss implications for nursing.

The provision of health care is a service. As such, it costs money. Many people believe health care is a right; however, defining the exact level of health care that should be guaranteed each citizen is a controversial subject that has not yet been resolved in the United States. Health is such a valuable and diversely defined commodity that it is difficult, if not impossible, to derive a standard pricing and payment scheme for providing health-related services. This issue is complicated by the challenge of constrained financial resources that may be devoted to health care. As a result, many avenues exist for financing and delivering care. In the United States, these mechanisms have changed markedly over the past 50 years.

Factors Leading to Changes in Health Care Financing and Delivery

Health care financing is influenced primarily by social expectations, economic trends, technological developments, and political factors. It is helpful to review factors contributing to alternative financing and delivery structures to give context to current debates (Azzahir et al. 1995, Sprenger 1995):

- Current system lacks coherence and convenience for its users.
- Funding flows through narrowly defined categories (e.g., diagnosis-related categories) that often ignore other significant effects of influence.
- Health services are often designed to address a crisis rather than to prevent one.
- No single entity or mechanism exists for evaluating the effectiveness of services, especially when services come from multiple providers.
- Marketplace is calling for a change.
- New markers and outcomes of success are emerging.

- Traditional, fragmented delivery system cannot provide the accountability now being demanded by consumers, employer groups, and payers.
- Buyers are searching for delivery systems that can manage the totality of care (from preventive to tertiary services) in a coordinated way.

The response to these factors has been the emergence of new mechanisms to finance and deliver care. Managed care and capitation strategies continue to sweep the health care horizon. Because capitation represents a departure from the traditional method of financing care, a brief overview of fee-for-service and prospective payment systems will be presented. The next section will provide an introduction to capitation within a historical context. Next, integrated delivery systems are described because they represent yet another step in the evolution of capitated care.

Fee for Service

Fee-for-service health care has been the traditional system of payment in the United States. This type of payment mechanism was characterized by patients directly paying for services provided by the physician or other health care provider. Under fee-for-service care, each encounter with a provider, procedure, test performed, or diagnosis made was traditionally reimbursable under a determined price structure.

Although fee-for-service payment prevailed for a significant length of time, changes in the health care system have led to alternative financing structures. Critics of fee for service note that it holds little incentive for cost-containment because providers are paid for each service rendered, which may sometimes result in overservice (Raffel and Raffel 1994). Additionally, patients may perceive that "more is better" even when this may not be the case, thus increasing the incentives to overuse services.

Factors that traditionally supported fee-for-service care are undergoing changes. These factors and current trends are outlined in the following paragraphs.

Information Asymmetry

In most business transactions, the buyer and seller are equally informed about the product. For instance, during the purchase of a refrigerator the buyer and seller possess essential information about price and quality of the item. Historically, this has not been the case in the health care market. Physicians and other providers maintained and guarded the knowledge base undergirding medical practice. Diseases and medications have Latin or unpronounceable names, leaving the patient at a disadvantage in understanding the "product" being exchanged. Similarly, health care jargon sometimes leaves the patient at a disadvantage in understanding his or her clinical situation. Very little information is available about price or quality in health care transactions. Because the patient is at an information disadvantage, comparing services between providers is difficult. This situation is known as asymmetry of information (Starr 1982).

Now, employer groups are a major intermediary between patients and providers in negotiating cost and quality. Employer groups have strongly encouraged health plans to provide information about quality and cost. Employer groups provided a major force behind the HEDIS (Health Plan Employer Data and Information Set) and continues to be a motivator for health plans to provide information about numerous quality indicators to purchasers.

Some argue that the emerging role of information technologies will provide patients with more information about the price and quality of their health care. The advent of published outcome reports and computer technologies, including widespread access to the World Wide Web, has given patients increased access to health care information. Patients may come to the health care encounter with information gleaned from a number of electronic sources. Some health care leaders predict these trends will decrease asymmetry of information and make quality and pricing data more readily available. An emerging role for nursing is to help patients become knowledgeable and critical consumers of information from a variety of sources.

Health Care as a Benefit of Employment

An important change in health care financing and insurance occurred when employers started offering health care coverage as part of the benefit package that they could offer to their employees. In many cases, attractive benefit packages were offered instead of increasing wages. Employers benefit because the tax treatment of health benefits is such that employer contributions for health insurance benefits are exempt from federal and state income taxation. There were two major consequences. Individuals purchased more insurance than they otherwise would have without the subsidy and more extensive health insurance resulted in increased health care spending (Manning et al. 1987).

Health care as an employment benefit changed the health care market immensely. Payment moved beyond a buyer-seller market where the patient directly purchased services to one where insurance companies often were the intermediary for the transaction. For several decades, fee for service worked as an operational and arguably effective payment methodology, with patients paying premiums and deductibles to the insurance company, which in turn paid for claims processed after a care transaction had taken place.

Specialization of Medical Practice

At the same time that insurance companies were playing a more active role in health care, the infrastructure of medicine was becoming more technology-intensive, leading to a tremendous move toward specialization. After World War II, medical technology proliferated rapidly. This momentum increased during the 1960s, fueled partly by the space race and the desire to compete technologically with other nations. This social value extended into health care. Private and public funds were poured into technological innovation. As new interventions became available, public demand for these procedures (e.g., CAT scans, magnetic resonance imagery, internal fetal monitoring) grew. As a result of this technology and related consumer demand, health care costs rose dramatically and continue to spiral upward.

Institutionalization of Health Care

A significant move from solo physician practices to group or corporate practices started after World War II. At first, this move was protested by organized medicine, but the advantages and economies of scale that were gained by practicing in groups were quite compelling (Starr 1982). As capitation became more pervasive, the move in the direction of group practice also continued. Generally, groups of providers are better able to negotiate contracts with managed care organizations than are solo practitioners.

The enactment of Medicare and Medicaid legislation in 1965 prompted the development of investor-owned hospital chains and assisted in the growth of university medical centers. The result was increased movement from solo, or community-based, practice to more corporate or academic centers for physicians and nurses. In addition, the education of physicians and nurses became centered on hospital-based training experiences. Each of these social trends had the effect of moving health care out of the community setting and into corporate centers, teaching hospitals, and large group practices. The effect was "institutionalizing" health care, or making the delivery of care somewhat dependent on the physical structure within which services were located (Starr 1982).

These and other developments in health care set the stage for a dramatic change in the way care was financed. There became a need to link financing with delivery structures in a manner that made patients and providers more accountable for cost containment. Capitation has evolved, in part, because of problems arising with traditional methods of health care financing.

Trends Supporting the Transition from Fee-For-Service to Prospective Payment

Physicians in private practice traditionally billed patients directly for services they provided. In the early 20th century, physicians introduced the concept of prepaid group practice, known as managed medical care delivery. This type of health care delivery was a precursor to prospective payment schemes. It was slow to catch on nationally, and resistance to the model was often intertwined with objections to a single payer system for health services and universal health care (Starr 1982, MacLeod 1995).

Retrospective payment refers to compensation for services after the service is provided. Hospitals and physicians traditionally were paid retrospectively. Indemnity insurance payment structures supported this system. Claims were submitted to the insurance company, then payment went to the hospital or physician. Some insurance programs paid for whatever the hospital or physician charged. In most cases, charges were higher than costs, which contributed to inflated total health care costs.

Retrospective payment mechanisms did not encourage cost containment or efficiency. Financial incentives existed for hospitals and physicians to encourage service utilization because insurance companies would pay for services used. Patients were not encouraged to manage health care consumption because they paid a standard premium and deductible no matter what services were used. Under this system, Medicare costs soared and the program's financial solvency was brought into question. These developments spurred investigation into prospective payment strategies.

Beginning in 1972, several demonstrations were funded to investigate a variety of alternative payment mechanisms. Prospective payment systems (PPS) were chosen as a way to try to contain inpatient Medicare costs, and in 1983 Congress amended the Social Security Act to pay for hospitalizations on a predetermined, diagnosis-specific rate. DRGs were phased in over a four-year period and have had implications for health care far beyond Medicare payment (Raffel and Raffel 1994).

The primary purpose of PPS was to change financial incentives by offering strong encouragement to reduce hospital costs. Under PPS, a hospital benefits if it can care for patients at a cost less than the allocated DRG. If the cost of care exceeds the DRG, however, the hospital loses money unless it can provide "outlier" documentation and justify additional payment (Raffel and Raffel 1994).

Despite reports of decreased hospital discharges (and therefore admissions) and length of stay, concern developed that hospitals were discharging patients too early. Referrals to home care agencies and skilled nursing facilities were fragmented in many cases, and discharge planners were faced with shortages of skilled nursing beds. The demand for ambulatory and outpatient care rose under DRGs. The debate concerning impacts on cost, quality, and continuity of care under prospective payment continues (Raffel and Raffel 1994).

Capitation

Before launching into a discussion about capitation, it is important to note that the following is a description of the ideas and principles of capitation and not an operational guide for how capitation appears in the "real world." Capitation takes on many forms, the diversity of which is well beyond the scope of this monograph. It is important, however, to understand the characteristics that make capitation different from fee-for-service health care, and those distinctions provide the focus for this section.

Capitation is a mechanism for linking financing with the delivery of care. In its simplest form, capitation is a set amount of money received or paid based on membership rather than services used or provided. Currently, capitation is replacing fee for service as the primary method of payment for health services (Kongstvedt 1995), and it has been advanced as a way to help manage health care expenditures.

Perhaps capitation is best understood by comparing it with fee-for-service care. In contrast to fee-for-service care, where health services are provided and paid for according to episodes of care, capitation focuses on providing care for populations over time. Under capitation, a fixed dollar amount is made available to the organization to provide or arrange for care for a group of individuals for a predetermined period. Capitation also involves shifting financial risk from payers to insurers and providers.

Capitation changes the logic for all stakeholders in health care, including patients, providers, and payers. Traditional performance measures under fee for service included market share (e.g., number of admissions, number of procedures, and number of visits) and costs (per procedure or stay), and management was focused on maintaining a high hospital occupancy rate. In contrast, performance measures under capitation are defined differently. For instance, market share is measured by the number of covered lives, costs are calculated differently (cost per life, inpatient days per 1,000, and visits per 1,000), and the management focus is on securing a low hospital occupancy rate and ensuring the correct modality of care. This means making sure patients see the most appropriate provider, in the right setting, and receive the right care (Spitzer-Lehmann 1996).

The move from fee-for-service care to capitated delivery systems requires a drastic change in thinking. These philosophical changes are summarized as follows (Sprenger 1995):

Traditional	*Capitation*
Patient model	Population-based
Illness/curative	Preventive/wellness
Tracking beds, admits	Tracking health status/outcomes
Service use generated revenue	Service use increases costs

Proponents of capitation have made some basic assumptions about the movement from fee for service to capitation. Predictions concerning this new payment system are tied to the following assumptions (Sprenger 1995):

- Traditional, fragmented delivery system will not stand the rigors of an organized buyer system (e.g., under a one payer system).
- Traditional system functions "boutique" style, with patients accessing care from several providers; accountability is difficult to establish in this type of system.
- Aligned financial incentives are required to access opportunities and to successfully manage provider "behaviors."

Health care policymakers, researchers, and practitioners have made the following general predictions about the future of health care under capitation (Sprenger 1995):

- Providers will accept financial risk under a range of contracted payment methods.
- Revenue centers will become cost centers.

- Most individuals will be covered by managed care systems (including Medicare and Medicaid beneficiaries).
- As managed care markets mature, they will move from discount to risk sharing.
- Non-traditional partnerships will develop.
- Physicians will seek larger integrated service models as preferred employment platforms.
- Cost shifting will be eliminated.

In some of the more mature managed care markets, these predictions have already become reality. As managed care markets evolve, new methods of capitation rate calculation and negotiation have emerged. Many nurse administrators, entrepreneurs, and consultants have been actively involved in developing new approaches of delivering quality care products while ensuring financial viability. Nurses must be aware of the changing financial incentives under capitation in order to identify new opportunities for career enrichment.

Integrated Systems

Some health planners predict that capitation will lead to a more integrated system of health care delivery as financial incentives change. As risk is shared more equally among patients, providers, and payers, the balance of power and responsibilities is likely to change. Proponents of integrated health care systems maintain that all involved parties will encounter new reasons to collaborate to ensure continuous, high quality care. Critics note that economic incentives will exert overwhelming pressures to compromise the quality of care. Suggested market consequences of capitation include the following (Sprenger 1995):

- Integration of care versus autonomous providers practicing in isolation;
- Inter/intra professional collaboration;
- Changes in the relationships among providers, plans, and payers of health care, resulting in diminished hostility and adversarial relationships; and
- Enhanced purchaser power.

Integration can have the effect of pooling resources and decreasing risk to individual providers. In addition, integrated systems have the purchasing power to contract with other providers to supply services the system itself would find too costly to develop. Integrated systems require a high level of accountability within the system and contracted providers. It has been predicted that accountable systems will (Sprenger 1995)

- Integrate providers,
- Provide or arrange for a full continuum of care,
- Assume and manage financial risk, and
- Provide cost-effective, price competitive, high quality outcomes.

Markets go through various stages of evolution as they mature, and the emphasis of risk changes as MCOs develop. These steps parallel the financing mechanisms outlined in this chapter: fee for service, prospective payment, capitation, and systems integration. The four major stages of market maturity are summarized in the following list (Eddy and Malcolm 1995, 30–35):

- *Stage One:* The delivery system is generally in a fee-for-service and discounted medicine phase. The guiding theme is based on the institutional mission statement and care is patient focused. Clinical quality outcomes are based on inpatient parameters (e.g., length of stay) and governance comes from institutional leadership.
- *Stage Two:* At this stage, the delivery system is characterized by managed payment and is guided by the integrated system. Patient care is member focused, and the outcomes are based on functional status and health outcomes. Leadership comes from the system level.
- *Stage Three:* The delivery system is now in an organized care framework. The operational focus is on the enrolled population, and clinical quality is measured by functional status or health outcomes, the same as in the previous stage. Clinical leadership guides the system.
- *Stage Four:* The delivery system is now focused on accountability, especially at the community level, with the operational focus being on community health. The guiding theme is based on community values. Clinical quality is measured by community health outcomes. Community leadership guides the delivery of health care.

Health plans with limited experience may focus solely on utilization constraints or prevention strategies with enrollees to contain costs, but more established MCOs have found this approach to be short-sighted for a number of reasons. Focusing on utilization constraints, limiting the amount or intensity of services, and delaying or preventing health services utilization may work in certain cases, but they are not generally successful in managing the health of a population over the long term. Instead, more mature managed care strategies are establishing community-centered approaches that target the values, health resources, constraints, capacities, and limitations of communities (Eddy and Malcolm 1995).

Accountability to the community stems from recognizing that members or enrollees do not exist in isolation from the communities in which they live. Health risks of the community affect individual members and groups of members, thereby affecting the health outcomes of the MCO (Eddy and Malcolm 1995). One of the most promising features for the profession of nursing that has emerged from managed care is the focus on community health.

Implications for Nursing

In conclusion, the challenges for a new health care financing system can be summarized by reflecting on a few core questions. Answering these questions thoughtfully and responsibly presents a timely challenge for nurses (Azzahir et al. 1995).

- What is the role of reimbursement? What do we pay for now? What services should we pay for? Are the results short- or long-term?
- What is the role of the delivery system? What level of care can be accessed in the hospital, clinic, and emergency department? Who qualifies for this care? How do we decide?
- What is the role of clinical guidelines? How can they be implemented and evaluated? Who is accountable?

- What is the role of revenue/cost? How does money flow through the health plan versus the delivery system?
- How can we measure success? In the past, revenue meant sick people in the delivery system. Can we move to revenue generated by healthy people in the community? How do we guard against barriers to care for those who need it?

Historically, nurses were not involved in the financing of health care. Nursing salaries were not connected to patient care; nurses were employed and paid by physicians, hospitals, or clinics. Therefore, when these entities came under the pressure of cost containment, nurses felt the financial impact indirectly. Now these changes are more direct, as evidenced by downsizing, movement of nursing career opportunities into the community, and population-based health care systems.

Changes in health care delivery have led to substantial growth in the home health and ambulatory care sectors. As a result, nurses have become much more aware and knowledgeable about financing issues. This will continue as capitation and integrated delivery systems continue to proliferate. Changes in Medicare and managed care reimbursement have had a huge impact on home health, hospice, and ambulatory care nursing. Along with the higher acuity patient population that was evidenced in the 1980s and early 1990s, these organizations are now experiencing new constraints on reimbursement. This has resulted in restructuring and downsizing efforts in these sectors as well as acute care settings.

The transition to capitation has had a side effect of highlighting the need for prevention, health education, longitudinal patient tracking, early detection of illness, and planning care for groups of patients. MCOs have invested in strategies to keep their covered population healthier to decrease the potential for higher future utilization and expenditures. Providing the resources for health screening, risk identification and reduction, community education, and health promotion are skills nurses have traditionally held and are strongly embedded in the history of the profession.

As financial incentives change, nurses must wear several hats. Nurses will continue to be patient advocates, focusing on groups and populations as well as individual patients. Ethical concerns will continue to surface, especially about health plans withholding treatment or not covering certain procedures. Nurses will be called upon to integrate fiscal responsibility with clinical care. These issues and changes may not be clear cut or fully visible, so nurses must be prepared as critical thinkers, able to focus on several aspects of complex problems.

Although restructuring trends have sometimes cost nurses jobs, some career opportunities are emerging in the new health arena. Recent reports have highlighted the substantial need for nurses now and in the future, particularly in community-based and ambulatory settings (U.S. Department of Health and Human Services 1993, 5–11; Pew Health Professions Commission 1995, 5–9). In fact, the report from the Department of Health and Human Services states that "nursing and nursing education are being challenged to provide for the increases in demand for baccalaureate-prepared professional nurses and master's prepared advanced practice nurses in non-hospital settings." However, the need for nurses documented in these reports is for specific practice realms such as ambulatory and community-based systems. A particular need for advanced practice nurses points to the need for educational models that re-tool the existing nurse workforce and facilitate movement through the different levels of nursing.

These reports are somewhat critical of the current system of multiple entry points into practice (associate, diploma, and baccalaureate) and recommend different levels of responsibility for each level of nursing. The U.S. Department of Health and Human Services report points out, "The percent of graduates earning baccalaureate degrees has remained about the same, while the percent of associate degrees has risen to represent about two-thirds of all graduates. The irony of this trend is that future demand for nurses will be oriented toward the baccalaureate prepared nurse" (U.S. Department of Health and Human Services 1993). The majority of new opportunities lie in ambulatory, primary, and community-based care settings rather than the hospital. Nursing practice, education, and research must reflect this emerging trend.

Population-Based Managed Care

MCOs are focusing their attention on improving care for groups of patients or subpopulations with common health care needs such as diabetics, pregnant teenagers, and patients with multiple sclerosis (Graff et al.1995, Shamansky 1996). Population-based care has been conceptualized as the development and implementation of a plan for the care of all patients with a specific clinical need or diagnosis (Wagner 1996). Demand management is a type of population-based care. It ideally involves providing a program that includes the following components: a registry of patients with the specified condition, a clear clinical course to be followed, carefully delineated outcomes, patient and provider training, centralized service delivery resources, and information systems for monitoring care (Wagner 1996).

There are generally two levels of population-based care. The first is the organizational level, in which the health plan or health care organization has the infrastructure in place to implement population-based care. The second is the individual practice level, in which clinicians are guided by information about their specific patient panels (Wagner 1996). A third, community-focused, level of population-based care is evolving. Some health care futurists have predicted that MCOs will need to move beyond enrollees to focus on the total community as the actual unit of change (Sprenger 1995).

Population-based care draws on theoretical approaches and data collection tools from several disciplines, including epidemiology, biostatistics, decision analysis, total quality management, cost-benefit analysis, and management theory. Surveys, focus groups, and clinical data collection provide information vital to population-based care strategy development (Shamansky 1996).

Why the Movement to Population-Based Care?

There are compelling reasons to create systems of care to manage subpopulations of patients. These include high costs associated with treating the complications of poorly managed illnesses and the frequency of preventable hospitalizations related to acute complications. Other reasons for the movement toward population-based care include (Shamansky 1996)

- Documented widespread variation in practice behavior associated with subsequent variation in patient outcomes;
- High rates of cost inflation;
- Purchasers who are demanding outcomes, guidelines, and data; and
- Clinicians who are asking for assistance in providing consistent, evidence-based care to their patients.

The goals of population-based care include (Shamansky 1996)

- Maximizing health outcomes and lowering costs for defined populations;
- Ensuring delivery of effective services;
- Eliminating ineffective services;
- Optimizing provider behavior toward meeting these goals; and
- Monitoring services and outcomes.

Steps to Implementing Population-Based Care

1. Choose and define a subpopulation. This can be done by age category (elderly), gender (depressed males), health status (patients with functional disabilities), pathologies (diabetes), lifestyle (smokers), or complaints (low back pain). The subpopulation should account for a significant portion of the clinical workload or cost. In addition, the subpopulation should be chosen for the probability that the clinical intervention will make a significant difference. Another important criterion is that the condition should respond to preventive measures (Shamansky 1996).
2. Identify services targeted to the subpopulation. Evidence-based care is the foundation of population-based managed care, so

a thorough review of the scientific literature and established practice guidelines should be conducted to determine state-of-the-art care for the subpopulation (Shamansky 1996).
3. Define the desired outcome(s) and design outcome(s) measures.
4. Plan for service delivery to the subpopulation.
5. Evaluate outcomes and adapt care strategies to continue improved care.
6. Make data available to clinicians in forms that are useful, concise, and adaptable to query by clinicians.

Expanded Roles for Nursing in Population-Based Care

Population-based care requires expanded nursing skills and roles. Graff et al. (1995) describe the major elements of care provided by nurses in expanded roles. Those that apply to population-based care include

- Analysis of health services and systems in terms of accessibility, sensitivity to patient needs, and cost-effectiveness for the target population;
- Design, direction, implementation, and evaluation of programmatic, technological, and educational directions for specified populations;
- Care coordination across the health–illness continuum, across settings, and beyond geographic boundaries;
- Consideration of organizational, community, and cultural implications of events and decisions related to care coordination;
- Emphasis on networks of providers, colleagues, and resources;
- Enhanced relationships with patients and providers as a result of clearly defining and demonstrating the contribution of nursing to the consumer's health;
- Emphasis on interdependent learning, open dialogue, collaboration, and a collective sense of responsibility; and
- Support of organization-wide, ongoing processes to improve service, clinical outcomes, and satisfaction.

Nurses in population-based care establish systems of care coordination for a specified subpopulation of patients. This system spans the health care continuum and covers all points in the spectrum of health–illness. Nurses may collaborate with physician colleagues in improving care for specified subpopulations (Graff et al. 1995). Roles and responsibilities for the expanded role of nurses in Graff's study included the following:

- Identifying at-risk populations;
- Developing interventions to reduce risk factors;
- Establishing care coordination systems;
- Ensuring the system spans the care continuum and health–illness spectrum;
- Creating resource networks and critical linkages for patients and staff to ensure access to needed services;
- Collecting, monitoring, and analyzing data;
- Identifying strategies to reduce hospital length of stay;
- Focusing on outcomes and reviewing variances from standards of care; and
- Using data to improve care and outcomes across the population.

Outcomes of population-based care can include, but are not limited to, the following (Graff et al. 1995):

- Increase in utilization of evidence-based guidelines;
- Decrease in hospitalizations;
- Decrease in inappropriate, unplanned provider visits;
- Increase in planned visits for preventive or routine care;
- Decrease in complications secondary to condition;
- Increase in patient satisfaction;
- Increase in patient self-management; and
- Increase in provider satisfaction.

Population-based care is one way to take full advantage of the structural components in place under managed care (an enrolled patient panel, links with primary care providers, and integrated financial and clinical information systems). Some health care needs are predictable; population-based care organizes strategies to make the most effective use of health care resources.

Self-Care Management and Self-Efficacy

Nursing has long advanced the idea that health is best supported by patients caring for themselves to the greatest extent possible. Patient self-efficacy skills training is important in illness management (Holman and Lorig 1992, 305–323). Self-care management is the ability of the patient to carry out behaviors that support health or to arrange care. Self-efficacy is defined as the individual's belief and self-confidence that he or she is capable of providing or arranging for a large portion of care targeted toward illness (Holman and Lorig 1992). In this sense, self-care management implies behaviors, whereas self-efficacy conveys self-confidence in one's abilities related to care.

Role of the Patient in Managed Care

Some managed care systems have placed a greater emphasis on self-management and lifestyle implications of disease. Management of health across the lifespan and across settings requires active participation and communication between the patient and health care provider to a larger extent than usual in traditional health care systems. As a result, outcome measures must be developed that capture the patient's participation as well as provider input (Lewis 1995).

A major theme emerging in health care is that the patient must be involved to the fullest possible extent in decision making for health care and services. Traditionally, clinicians "provided" care and patients "received" it, as if health care were a commodity. The process of providing and receiving care, however, was never a normal market situation because the clinicians always had more information about the illness or condition than the patient. This placed the patient in a passive role. Managed care models represent a departure from this traditional way of thinking in that they empower the patient through information sharing. However, some patients are better equipped for this role than others.

A primary challenge in health care is helping patients make informed choices relative to their care and ensuring that patients understand the personal impact of these choices. This challenge is particularly compelling with at-risk or frail individuals or those with multiple conditions because information, delivery systems, and care strategies are more complex and harder to navigate when caring for a constellation of conditions and lifestyle patterns.

Health care professionals must continue to pay close attention to patients' preferences, lifestyle patterns, and unique individual characteristics. Patients are the only ones who can provide the health care team with a clear perspective stemming from their individual vantage point. Patients attribute unique meanings to their health, illness, and life patterns. These meanings shape the way care is delivered within the health care framework.

Clinicians who listen to patients and genuinely regard them as an integral part of the team also will be open to the mutual learning that can occur as part of the team process. Patients in these teams are more likely to share their self-care strategies, barriers to instituting care plans, and progress on team goals. The foundation for this sharing is a high level of trust between individuals.

Patient-focused care requires a new orientation to care on the part of patients as well as nurses. This means letting go of traditional role expectations and preparing for different ways of communicating, participating, and evaluating care. For instance, clinicians no longer do things "to" or "for" patients, but rather work with them to acomplish mutual goals and learning.

Patient self-management offers the patient more choices and provides participative guidance in navigating the choices. Often, patients enter the health care arena at a decision point: The strategies they have been using to care for themselves are no longer adequate; thus they are faced with not only illness, but also the choice of how to proceed. A characteristic of managed care that complicates this process is that insurance coverage sometimes affects the options available to patients.

Accessing the health care system allows clinicians to work with the patient to identify and define the issue(s), describe a realistic goal, and arrive at a plan to reach the goal. Open communication is a vital component of this relationship. A fear that MCOs would dictate the amount and type of information providers could give patients about treatment options was the motivation behind legislation designed to ban "gag orders." Gag orders theoretically could be used to limit the amount of information a provider could give to patients concerning various treatment options.

Implications for Nursing

Population-based care holds great potential for the discipline of nursing. Central concepts in nursing, such as accurate health assessment, planning, and evaluation, are especially crucial in caring for patient aggregates. Health promotion and disease prevention are activities nurses are well qualified to execute. Planning health interventions for groups has long been a focus of public health and community health nursing. Evaluation based on sound statistical data provides opportunities for nurse administrators, researchers, and consultants. Interpreting patterns and trends in the data in terms of human response to illness and well-being is a charge nurses must be well equipped to face.

An example of nurses using population-based reporting to identify care needs in team practice is the Geriatric Collaborative Model implemented by the Carle Clinic Association with support from the John A. Hartford Foundation and the Carle Foundation. The model places patients, primary care physicians, and nurse partners in teams for care delivery targeted to meet the needs of the geriatric subpopulation. Nurses care for panels of patients and receive information about demographics, health status, health conditions, functional status and medications on individual patients, and patient aggregates. The nurse and physician work together to identify patterns in the information reports and address unmet needs accordingly (Schraeder, Shelton, Britt, Dworak, Fraser, and Grimes 1997; Shelton et al. in press).

Nurses must be simultaneously observers and participants in the patient care encounter, bringing clinical expertise to the situation, but not overshadowing patients' views and experience. The belief undergirding patient self-management is that individuals can participate in their own care by choosing resources that best meet their individual needs. The concept is to couple increased choices with the information related to those choices, believing that the consuming public can make sound decisions when armed with options and information. This idea has long been embraced by the discipline of nursing.

5

Risk Models

CHAPTER OBJECTIVES

- Define risk.
- Explain who holds the risk in managed care.
- Describe how risk is shared in managed care.
- Explore incentives tied to risk.
- Highlight implications of risk sharing for nursing.

Historical, structural, and financial aspects of managed care were presented in Chapters 2 and 3. Basic principles of population-based care were introduced in Chapter 4. The interrelationships among these basic concepts provide the foundation for understanding the implications of financial risk and risk sharing. Risk is an essential element that differentiates managed care from traditional, fee-for-service health care delivery strategies.

What is Risk?

Traditional indemnity insurance, coupled with fee-for-service reimbursement, placed insurers at financial risk. Capitation theoretically has the effect of spreading financial risk across all parties: providers, payers (insurers), and patients. Risk, in this sense, is defined as the financial accountability for paying for health care services rendered. There are also legal and ethical components related to accountability for care provided, but in this chapter the discussion will center on the financial risks under capitation.

Capitation may seem a lucrative payment model, especially when patient panels consist of primarily healthy individuals. Most provider panels, however, also include a number of chronically or catastrophically ill members. These individuals require more intensive, closely coordinated care and services for a longer duration. In short, their care costs much more to deliver. How do MCOs manage care for their sicker enrollees while maintaining financial viability? The key to financial success under capitation is to distribute risk to a large and diverse membership panel. MCOs need to have membership panels that include enough healthy individuals to balance the care and cost for the less healthy.

This need for economies of scale has encouraged creative alliances between providers, hospitals, and community services with the goal of managing their individual and collective risks under capitation (Miles 1997). Allocation of resources on the basis of need is a difficult task, primarily because need is so hard to define. This has led to closer examination of risk screening procedures, clinical practice patterns, standards of care, and observable outcomes.

Who Holds the Risk?

A major theme of managed care is that financial risk must be shared between health care providers and insurers in order to contain costs and manage service utilization. Patients also share part of this risk by virtue of being affected by this restructuring of the delivery system. Although patients assume more of the risk under managed care, optimal patient participation in the model has not yet been realized. This may change as consumer information about health plans and providers becomes more accessible to patients.

Risk-sharing pools are used by MCOs in various forms. No single form has emerged as ideal. Generally, risk-sharing pools involve the allotment of a fixed amount (pool) of money from which specified services are paid through the contract period (usually a year). The funds remaining at the end of the contracted period are divided between the providers and the insurer. Frequently, separate risk pools are created for physician and hospital services and they typically do not include medical specialists who are used on a referral basis (Williams and Torrens 1993).

The principal idea underlying the use of risk pools is to provide an incentive to reduce use, especially hospitalizations and referrals to specialists. Questions remain about the effectiveness of risk pools in accomplishing this goal. The issue of whether risk pools result in underuse of necessary services is also receiving increased investigation.

Shift of Risk

Managed care has dramatically changed the risk structure of health care. Instead of providers being reimbursed for services rendered, they often are paid on a capitated basis or flat salary. In this sense, they share the financial risk with the insurer. If providers authorize or deliver health services without managing costs, they pay the financial consequences.

A major trend emerging in managed care risk sharing is stop-loss protection for provider organizations. Stop-loss protection is a measure that defines the level of financial risk to which a provider is exposed and protects individual providers from extraordinary risk. This protection may be built into the contract by the insurer as stop-loss insurance. The insurer has a very real financial interest in making sure providers are solvent and satisfied with the contract. Of course, payers want to ensure the best possible prices from providers, but ultimately the insurer benefits when providers are satisfied (Kongstvedt 1995, Williams and Torrens 1993).

Incentives Tied to Risk

Financial risk and incentives are different sides of the same coin. Risk is the threat of what will happen if care is not managed in a financially responsible manner, and incentives are the benefits as perceived by each of the parties involved. The risks and incentives under managed care continue to evolve as new methods for managing care emerge.

Fee-for-service medicine created incentives for overwork by providers and overutilization of services. Malpractice suits helped foster the use of defensive medicine, which also contributed to overuse and higher insurance costs. These costs were ultimately passed on to the consumer. Consumers were inclined to use as many services as they wanted from as many providers as they wanted, within limits, for a fixed premium. The incentives that built the fee-for-service infrastructure are reversed under managed care.

The incentive for the insurer is to enroll a stable and known patient population, maintain a core of qualified providers, and keep enrollee satisfaction levels high. The providers are encouraged to practice preventive medicine, manage a panel of patients over time, and effectively manage service use and cost. Employer groups have an incentive to contract with MCOs that provide high patient satisfaction and contain costs so the employer group can offer competitive benefit options to its employees. Patients have a financial incentive to seek preventive and primary care (low or no co-payments) and access care through a gatekeeper (otherwise payment is denied). In reality, these incentives are sometimes blurred, hidden, and have the tendency to change rapidly.

Risk Sharing: System Issues

Capitation places health care providers and plans at financial risk. The allotment of funds used to care for individuals is finite, and must be well managed in order to sustain high quality care for all enrollees while providing for financial success of the plan, group, or providers. Capitation usually occurs at the system level. There becomes a need to align incentives of patients, providers, and payers in order to achieve success. This requires a new emphasis on integration, not shifting risk, by aligning interests and providing a single point of accountabilities.

The following and other predictions have been made about the future effects of capitation (Sprenger 1995):

- Capitation methods will become more fully implemented at the systems level and will improve population-based care.
- Parties will share risks and rewards.
- Creation of rewards related to performance will be emphasized.
- Capitation rates will be designed that better reflect the population health status and include ways of identifying proper ratios of providers to patients.
- Need to support long-term partnerships among employer groups, MCOs, and communities will endure.
- Community-based health promotion and disease prevention will replace programs targeted only to enrollees.

Risk sharing in a capitated environment is a dynamic concept. The ideas presented here are more theoretical than the systems that are currently in operation. Organizational forms are evolving and changing so rapidly in health care that it would be difficult to accurately portray a typical capitated environment. New ways of operationalizing shared risk continue to emerge as provider networks grow and change. Risk sharing has several common attributes (Sprenger 1995):

- Accountability lies with prepaid enrollees.
- Broadened focus is needed on community and systems level interventions because concentration solely on individuals is not sufficient to affect long-range health outcomes.
- Totality of care must be managed, embracing both cost-effectiveness and quality.
- Prevention makes fundamental, long-term, business sense in capitation.

- Selection of health problems and definitions of communities will be prioritized by purchaser requirements, cost analysis, epidemiological analysis, and regulatory requirements.
- Strategies will go "upstream" into the determinants of health using primary, secondary, and tertiary prevention approaches at the individual, community, and systems level.
- Providers, MCOs, and patients must collaborate in order to achieve optimal results.

In summary, risk sharing is a major component that makes capitation vastly different from fee-for-service health care. Along with sharing financial risk, all parties become stakeholders in clinical outcomes as well. Risk sharing incorporates two essential elements of financial viability. The first is to increase the number of enrollees in order to spread the risk and avoid adverse selection. The second is to control high cost and ineffective treatment modalities (Spitzer-Lehmann 1996).

Implications for Nursing

Risk sharing creates an environment in which nurses can use established skills and gain new ones. For instance, nurses in care management roles can facilitate links among providers, MCOs, and patients by understanding and articulating the financial and clinical interests each party brings to the encounter. The traditional patient advocacy role for nurses is especially important because nurses can help patients identify and access covered services, negotiate the appeals process when necessary, and obtain required referrals to specialty care.

Nurses in community-based organizations and ambulatory care settings can help define and quantify risk by participating in the assessment of patient and population health needs. Examples of this function include examining patterns of preventive health measures, hospitalization rates, and average length of stay for defined patient panels. Nurse managers can use population-based health reports to manage staffing issues and inform budget decisions.

Nurses in management and administrative roles must be able to provide documentation of improved clinical outcomes that are directly related to nursing care. Often, nursing leaders are placed in the position of balancing "productivity" with patient acuity and constrained staffing abilities. In addition, understanding reimbursement patterns and budgetary constraints is a considerable challenge, particularly in the face of rapid and widespread change such as that seen in home health care. It is particularly beneficial for nurses to understand the complex and interwoven incentives within managed care.

When MCOs reach out to the community to determine and reduce high risk health practices, nurses can play a central role. Nurses are well equipped to define, measure, and manage outcomes data related to improving care strategies. An example is monitoring the health and preventive practices (e.g., mammography rates, flu shots, and immunization rates) of a defined population for compliance with national guidelines and perhaps advising new strategies to improve outcomes.

Another important role for nursing will be to help patients and health care providers monitor systems for potential incongruencies or conflicts of interest relating to patient care and financing. When the delivery and financing of care are linked, as they are in managed care, the potential increases for conflicts of interest. This is a well-documented source of controversy and has been called the "managed care backlash" (Blendon et al. 1998). Although the public wants managed costs, it also is wary of the impact of managed care on quality. Individual patients may request assistance from nurses in order to understand and access the health care system. When conflicts arise between services the patients want and those that are covered by the plan, patients may ask the nurse to help access the appeals process. To determine if these potential conflicts are genuine or more a reflection of a changing system, the nurse must be aware of the risks and incentives and must be prepared to help the patient negotiate the health care system or initiate the appeals process, or explain to them why certain services are not covered.

It should be noted that strong mechanisms for quality assurance are in place, and regulation of MCOs continues to grow. Managed care quality is heavily regulated at several levels, including by federal, state, and private organizations. Examples include oversight from the NCQA (National Committee for Quality Assurance), URAC (Utilization Review Accreditation Commission), as well as current legislation (President's Commission for Consumer Protection). The mechanisms for quality assurance stem from many levels. Nurses are quite active in many of these organizations.

Perhaps one of the most exciting aspects of risk sharing is what nursing can learn as new models continue to emerge, as well as the ways in which nurses may shape the way health care is delivered in the future. However, as providers, nurses also face the potential losses in financial and career opportunities inherent in risk sharing. As with most aspects of managed care and its implications for nursing, the news is not entirely bad or good, but rather a mixture of both.

No discussion of risk would be complete without mentioning the legal aspects of risk for nurses under managed care. New roles may bring responsibilities that nurses must be aware of in order to protect themselves from liability. For example, in some triage and utilization management roles, nurses may not see patients face-to-face, yet the nurse may have a strong impact on care decisions. Home health agencies also must be aware of legal requirements related to Medicare reimbursement for services and billing practices. Nurse practitioners providing care within MCOs must be aware of liability coverage issues. All of these examples point to the need for nurses to be knowledgeable about their state nurse practice laws and liability coverage (Britt 1998).

Recognition of the importance of health maintenance and prevention in population-based care affords many opportunities in nursing. To prosper in a capitated environment, nursing leaders must maintain a thirst for learning, ongoing persistence, keen awareness, and a willingness to be flexible (Spitzer-Lehmann 1996). Additionally, nurses must voice support, concern, and interest in relevant issues in order to shape the system into one that most optimally serves patients.

6

Utilization Management

CHAPTER OBJECTIVES

- Describe the four major themes of financial controls: primary care provider, utilization review, networks or associations between providers, and capitated reimbursement.
- Explain the different types of utilization review: retrospective, concurrent, and prospective.
- Describe the role of authorization in utilization management.
- Describe the role of case management in utilization management.
- Explain the potential of evidence-based clinical practice in decreasing costs.
- Highlight implications for nursing.

A major goal of managed care is to integrate financial and economic considerations into the clinical decision-making process. MCOs use a variety of mechanisms to manage costs, primarily through monitoring, limiting, and evaluating health service utilization. The particular utilization management strategies used will depend on the overall mission and organizational structure of the MCO. Usually, several approaches are employed to contain costs. Nurses play a comprehensive role in utilization management, case management, and managing quality, cost, and outcomes.

MCOs differ regarding how tightly they control these mechanisms. Four interventions have been identified as major means of controlling costs: primary care providers, utilization review, formation of networks and associations, and capitated financing (Landry and Knox 1996). To some degree, all four major cost control mechanisms have been applied in most MCOs.

Types of Financial Control

Four types of financial control discussed in this section are primary care provider, utilization review, formation of networks and associations, and capitated financing.

Primary Care Provider

Usually a physician, the PCP serves as the first point of access to care. In some systems, nurse practitioners also may act as the PCP, with physician support. All enrollees must choose or are assigned a PCP. This is the MCO's attempt to minimize inappropriate utilization by limiting the enrollee's ability to gain direct access to referral services such as medical specialists (Grimaldi 1996).

In the gatekeeper role, the PCP is responsible for determining what level and intensity of care is warranted and then authorizing the appropriate level of service. The gatekeeper function is intended to decrease or eliminate inappropriate patient self-referrals to specialists. The use of a PCP also has the goal of substituting less costly care when appropriate and avoiding unnecessary service use. Usually, unauthorized services will not be paid for by the MCO.

In tightly managed MCOs, all hospitalizations must be authorized and the PCP is required to manage the care of hospitalized patients, even if most of the care is directly provided by specialists. In addition, tightly managed MCOs require PCP authorization for all encounters with specialists, not just the initial visit. Patients may self-refer to specialists or other providers out of the MCO's service network, but the MCO may refuse to pay all or part of the bills incurred (Grimaldi 1996).

Case management may serve as an adjunct to the PCP in cases in which service needs or utilization is intense or expected to continue for an extended time. Case management will be covered more thoroughly later in this chapter, but it is important to note that case managers sometimes function in the gatekeeping role. Here they may decide whether the care rendered to the enrollee is appropriate on two counts: clinical and financial.

Utilization Review

Utilization review is an evaluation technique to determine resource utilization patterns in patient care (Landry and Knox 1996). The objectives of utilization review are to establish cost control, promote quality of care, and encourage patient satisfaction (Taylor and Taylor 1994). Under fee-for-service financing, getting patients into the health care setting meant financial success. Under capitation, the opposite is true; success rests in ensuring that access and utilization are appropriate. This approach is monitored through utilization review.

To evaluate utilization, service use is usually tracked over time. Tightly managed MCOs usually rely on a unique identifying number for each authorization so that all services that are provided match exactly those that were authorized. This link requires an information system that allows comparisons between claims and authorizations (Grimaldi 1996).

Utilization review is meant to assure patients of appropriate care with appropriate resources. Theoretically, initial cost savings by an MCO are

usually tied to limits placed on hospital inpatient care. The money saved in this area can then be used to finance outpatient care or expand primary care services. Utilization review is the principal method of realizing a reduction in inpatient hospitalizations and length of stay. Traditional methods include preadmission certification, continued stay review, retrospective review, preadmission testing, same-day surgery, and targeted case management. Tightly controlled MCOs implement these methods more aggressively than traditional indemnity insurance plans (Grimaldi 1996).

There are three general types of utilization review:

1. *Retrospective:* This type of review takes place after the service is delivered. For example, a patient's chart is reviewed after hospitalization to evaluate the appropriateness of care given the specific circumstance.
2. *Concurrent:* Concurrent review occurs while the service is being provided. For example, a review of home health nursing visits takes place while the care is ongoing.
3. *Prospective:* Tightly managed MCOs prefer prospective utilization management, in which care maps are implemented to keep utilization on track with expected rates. Care is evaluated before it is rendered. For example, a patient planning a total hip replacement follows a critical pathway guiding pre-, peri-, and post- operative care. The pathway is evaluated and approved prior to its use.

Formation of Networks and Associations

Managed care organizations often form informal or contractual arrangements between care providers along the continuum from acute to long-term care. Financing, administration, and service delivery may be linked formally or informally. The objective of these networks is to provide integrated care that meets a variety of patient needs across the health care continuum. Although a single entity may not be able to provide all the services necessary for the health of its enrollees, it may contract for the provision of services with other providers.

Integrated delivery systems combine hospitals, physicians, and other providers and come in a variety of shapes, sizes, and structures. One type of integrated system is a physician hospital organization (PHO). Generally, PHO formation is initiated by hospitals to increase market share. Most PHOs are owned by hospitals, and thus have control over the board of directors. It is the board of directors that decides how capitation funds are divided among the hospital, physicians, and other providers (Bodenheimer and Grumbach 1996).

Capitated Financing

As described previously, capitated reimbursement is meant to limit financial risk to the MCO by shifting it to the health care provider. Capitation holds revenues constant by virtue of reimbursing the MCO a predetermined amount based on the number of enrollees. Because revenues are fixed, the health care provider can improve financial viability only through controlling costs.

MCOs manage cost-control processes more or less tightly, depending on the philosophy, structure, and capabilities of the individual organization. Capitation arrangements encourage MCOs to limit costs through limiting utilization. As a result, the more tightly managed utilization is, the more likely the MCO is to prevent unnecessary medical costs.

Role of Authorization in Utilization Management

Authorization processes are a critical component of managed health care. Authorization practices vary, as does the "tightness" of how authorization processes are managed. For instance, in one MCO authorization might be as simple as precertification of elective surgery, whereas in a more tightly managed MCO virtually all non-primary care processes might require preauthorization (Kongstvedt 1995).

Purposes of authorization (Kongstvedt 1995) are to

- Review a case for medical necessity,
- Channel the care to the most appropriate provider and setting,
- Provide information to concurrent utilization review and case management reporting systems, and
- Facilitate financial estimates of medical expenditures by providing a record of the services authorized by providers.

Many issues regarding authorization are specific to the MCO. These issues include specification of which services require authorizations, which providers/personnel can authorize services, and which services or procedures require special authorization from the MCO's medical director. The consensus is that the tighter the authorization system the more control the MCO has over utilization management (Kongstvedt 1995).

Following are the six general types of authorizations:

1. *Prospective (Precertification):* As the name indicates, this authorization is issued before any service is rendered. The time required between authorization and service use allows the MCO more knowledge and control of utilization. The medical director of the MCO may intervene if services seem inappropriate or excessive.
2. *Concurrent:* Authorizations are issued at the time services are delivered. This type of authorization allows for timely data collection, but provides the plan less of a chance to intervene before initial services are rendered.
3. *Retrospective:* Authorizations are issued after the service has already been delivered. MCOs generally agree to authorize emergency or out-of-state services retrospectively, but there also may be a high volume of retrospective authorizations for non-urgent services. Often, retrospective authorizations result from PCPs or other providers not following authorization protocols, which can be costly to the plan.
4. *Pended (For Review):* This situation occurs when an authorization is under evaluation for medical necessity or administrative review. It is unknown whether the authorization will be granted.
5. *Denial:* Denied authorizations are those for which the plan refuses to issue and pay.
6. *Subauthorization:* Authorization provides for a series of services to be covered under the initial authorization (e.g., anesthesia, pathology, and pharmacy) for hospitalization.

Authorization of services represents a major utilization control tool for MCOs. The particular authorization system and requirements depend on the individual MCO. Authorization data systems should help utilization managers track patterns and target areas for cost-effectiveness improvement.

Case Management

Case management programs are implemented in various ways, depending on the organizational goals, disciplinary focus, personnel, and setting. Case management has been defined many different ways, but the definition used here is "a collaborative process which assesses, plans, implements, coordinates, monitors, and evaluates options and services to meet an individual's health needs through communication and available resources to promote quality, cost-effective outcomes." [Case Management Society of America 1995 (excerpted with permission of the publisher)].

Comparison of Case Management and Utilization Management

Case management is a mechanism for matching the health care needs of a population to the appropriate use of health services, spanning the continuum of care. Although case management systems are often costly to initiate and maintain, they often promote health maintenance and decrease hospitalization rates. Since case management often results in cost-effective and coordinated care, it is sometimes confused with utilization review. Case management and utilization management are essentially different processes, although the two may have some overlapping aspects (U.S. Department of Health and Human Services 1996). In fact, in well-managed MCOs, utilization management and case management often overlap because utilization management can help identify at-risk patients.

Case management involves active identification of at-risk individuals or groups, focuses on the continuum of care, intervenes with a small number of individuals at a high level of intensity, and focuses on medically appropriate care. In contrast, utilization management does not focus on case-finding, but instead concentrates on patients who have already entered the health care setting (usually the acute care arena). In this way, utilization man-

agement has traditionally focused more on episodic care than on longitudinal care processes, targeted a large number of patients at a low level of intensity, and used prior authorization and concurrent review to manage service utilization and monitor medical necessity (Aliotta 1996, 61–72).

Comparison of Case Management and Managed Care

In addition to being associated with utilization management, case management is also often confused with managed care. Managed care is an overarching system that provides the infrastructure for managing use, cost, quality, and effectiveness of services. Case management is a mechanism for achieving more specific goals focused on care delivery and evaluation (Cohen and Cesta 1997).

Although case management and managed care may be theoretically distinct, they can be used simultaneously as mutually supportive processes. Indeed, they share many objectives and characteristics (Stetler 1987, Etheridge and Lamb 1989), including

- Facilitation of achievement of standardized patient outcomes;
- Assurance of appropriate length of stay;
- Promotion of appropriate utilization of resources;
- Promotion of collaborative practice, coordination, and continuity of care; and
- Direction of the contribution of all care providers toward the achievement of patient outcomes.

Components of Case Management Programs

Several major service components are found in most case management models (Weil and Karls 1985):

- Client identification and outreach,
- Individual assessment and diagnosis,
- Service planning and resource identification,
- Links between clients and needed services,
- Service implementation and coordination,
- Monitoring of service delivery,
- Advocacy, and
- Evaluation.

Case Management Goals

Case management probably will appear and operate differently in each health care institution, but the National Institute on Community-Based Long-Term Care has advanced the following care management goals (1990):

- Maintaining the greatest amount of independence and human dignity for the individual;
- Enabling the person to remain in the most appropriate environment;
- Providing an appropriate, comprehensive, and coordinated response to the person's need(s) that addresses prevention as well as rehabilitative maintenance;
- Serving as an integral link to increased access to community-based services;
- Building and strengthening family and community support;
- Improving the availability and quality of services;
- Reaching a specified target population;
- Containing costs by ensuring use of appropriate community-based services.

Additional goals may include

- Emphasizing prevention and patient/family education for self-management;
- Providing early outreach and monitoring health changes; and
- Providing professional nursing assessments and service coordination and delivery.

There are instances when these goals may be in conflict, especially if the case management program dwells within a managed care setting. Although these instances are rare, especially when decisions are based on clinical goals, it is important to recognize that they may occur. Potential conflicts can include (National Institute on Community-Based Long-Term Care 1990)

- Client and case manager disagree about the need or care plan;
- Family/client and case manager disagree about the appropriate plan and goals of care;
- Cost containment may limit the ability to be responsive to client needs and preferences; and

- Program goals do not coincide with the desire of the patient.

Nurses in case management and supervisory roles must be aware of these potential conflicts in order to identify and address them when they occur. In addition, the case manager may help the client and family negotiate the managed care system or appeal decisions regarding care. When in these situations it is important for the case manager to be alert to potential sources of role conflict deriving from simultaneous loyalty to the client and the MCO.

Many manuals, guides, and books have been written about nursing case management, including guidelines for implementing case management in different settings and with a variety of patient populations. Additional resources are included in the bibliography at the end of this monograph.

Case management represents a significant inroad for the future for nursing. Case management is a mechanism by which nurses can accomplish several important goals:

- Provision of coordinated care for patients and families;
- Movement toward the broader spectrum of caring for groups and populations of patients; and
- Demonstration of the cost-effectiveness of nursing care by measuring outcomes of case management.

Each of these aspects of nursing case management is rich with career possibilities. Insurers, employer groups, health care institutions, businesses, and outcomes management firms will continue to need individuals who can perform and develop nursing case management functions.

Potential of Evidence-Based Practice

Evidence-based clinical practice refers to guidelines or pathways that have been developed by expert opinion, literature review, or clinical trials. The movement toward designing, implementing, and evaluating evidence-based practice (EBP) has gained momentum over the past 15 years. The major goal of EBP is to standardize the processes and outcomes of care. Cost savings resulting from efficiency and adoption of best practices have been predicted to be a consequence of standardized care.

Initially, development of EBP guidelines was a response to the documentation of widespread, unexplainable, and significant variations in medical practice across defined geographic areas. This is known as small area variation. An example is a vastly different rate of angioplasty in two adjacent communities when all other factors are controlled for (e.g., patient demographics, number and types of hospitals, types of health insurance coverage). The existence of this unexplainable variation has been well studied and documented (Wennberg 1984).

The consequence of small area variations is that health service utilization is inconsistent, unpredictable, and much more expensive in some areas than others. Further, this inconsistency appears to have no direct relationship to patient need. When the literature on small area variations emerged simultaneously with alarming reports of spiraling medical costs, the federal government responded. Part of this response was the creation of the Agency for Health Care Policy and Research (AHCPR).

The AHCPR has been responsible for developing and disseminating an array of clinical guidelines for specific medical conditions. The guidelines are based on literature review and expert panel opinion. They outline steps that should ideally be followed when a patient presents with a particular diagnosis. Recently, AHCPR's mission has expanded to support research designed to improve the quality of health care, reduce its cost, and broaden access to essential services.

Many institutions also started developing specific guidelines, pathways, and standards of care. Again, the major goal was to standardize practice, but cost-effectiveness was predicted to follow. Investigations are ongoing about whether guidelines are effective in meeting these goals.

Implications for Nursing

The discipline of nursing has an opportunity to demonstrate the clinical and fiscal effectiveness of nursing care for individual patients as well as populations. Utilization management is a powerful mechanism for nurses to use their knowledge and skills in a way that targets care for patients that need it, decreases duplications in care, and evaluates efficiency of care strategies. Nurses possess a depth and breadth of clinical knowledge that can be used to make sound evaluations and recommendations.

Case management and the implementation of EBP are areas in which nurses can have significant clinical and financial impact. Designing, implementing, and evaluating case management programs and EBP are well within the realm of nursing care. In fact, many have pointed out that Florence Nightingale was truly a leader in EBP because of her emphasis on supporting practice with facts and statistics. These approaches benefit from collaboration with patients and professionals from other disciplines. In addition, nurses play critical roles in the development of best practices and clinical pathways that guide clinical care. Incorporating nursing care into practice guidelines also is an important area for nursing practice, education, and research.

Nurses bring a comprehensive focus to their roles in utilization management, case management, and optimizing quality, cost-effectiveness, and patient outcomes. Utilization management can benefit from a pragmatic balance between clinical and financial considerations.

Information Management

Information systems are a vital component of managed care approaches on two fronts: clinical and financial. It is not enough for nurses to have clinical and financial expertise; they also must have skills and knowledge about information systems (Simpson 1994). Information systems provide a crossroads for linking clinical delivery with financing structures because they can track market trends; access critical pathways, variances, and outcomes measurements; and generate required reports. In any discussion of information systems, confidentiality of patient information must be addressed. Nurses can play a vital role in bringing this issue to the table and help-ing develop systems that are appropriately sensitive to patient confidentiality.

Managed care, because it so closely links clinical and financial aspects of care, requires sound and timely use of information. At minimum, an operational information system should contain capabilities for utilization, quality measures, case management, specialty referral, prior authorization, patient access, member services, and patient and provider satisfaction (Stahl 1996).

Nursing Informatics

Nursing informatics is an area of critical importance and has grown substantially in the past two decades. The developmental path of nursing informatics runs parallel to advances in theory, research, and clinical information. This exponential growth in a changing health care environment provides a strong reason for developing information systems that demonstrate nursing's clinically meaningful and economically valuable contributions to patient care.

Information systems that track patient movement across the continuum of care and subsequent health outcomes are being carefully scrutinized by policymakers, payers, and consumers. Articulation of the clinical and financial worth of nursing care is essential. Sound management, processing, and transformation strategies are urgently needed for nursing data, information, and knowledge. Nurses must use their skills to help develop and use information technologies to benefit patient care, nursing theory development, and research.

Nursing informatics is the application of computer science, information science, and nursing expertise to the management, processing, and transformation of data, information, and knowledge to support nursing practice and the delivery of nursing care (Graves and Corcoran 1989). This branch of nursing science is concerned with clinical content at different levels of organization.

Data, information, and knowledge are the building blocks of informatics. For instance, data are discrete entities that can be described objectively, and information is data that have been interpreted, organized, or structured. Knowledge is information that has been synthesized so that interrelationships are identified and formalized. The highest level of abstraction is wisdom, or knowing when and how to use knowledge. Wisdom requires not only knowledge, but also values and experience (Joos et al. 1992, 221–225).

Data, information, knowledge, and wisdom are the nouns of informatics. Managing, processing, and transforming are the verbs. Managing is the functional ability to collect, aggregate, organize, move, and re-present information in an economical, efficient way that is meaningful to the users of the system. Processing is analogous to the processing that is done by nurses to make clinical decisions, by researchers to discover and verify knowledge, and by theorists to develop nursing theory. Transforming is the method of moving data or information to another, usually more complex, state of organization or meaning. For example, data are transformed to information, which is then transformed to knowledge and ultimately to wisdom (Amos and Graves 1989).

Major issues face nursing informatics. The first is that nursing deals with complex, dynamic, whole person phenomena that are difficult to capture in purely quantifiable terms. The second is that the discipline of nursing uses multiple conceptual frameworks. The third is that it is difficult to determine which data elements are required to capture different nursing diagnostic or classification systems, interventions, and outcomes. Measures must portray the multiple, inter-

acting facets of human nature rather than discrete, singular elements. There also is the "fuzzy" nature of clinical conditions. For example, relative terms such as tall, strong, and warm are all dependent on the context and clinical situation of the nurse and the patient (Graves and Corcoran 1989).

The mission of nursing informatics is to examine the structuring and processing of a growing body of health care information to arrive at clinical decisions and to build systems to support or automate that processing (Graves and Corcoran 1989). Accepted and standardized data sets and information systems are needed to document care across settings, classify nursing phenomenon, and allow for the common use of terms across disciplines (Werley, Devine, and Zorn 1988, Ryan and Delaney 1995). Ideally, systems should be compatible and built upon existing information systems.

Much of the existing work in nursing informatics has taken place in acute care and academic settings. However, there is a growing body of research on nursing informatics in community-based and managed care settings. With initiatives to move nursing care back into the community and out of the tertiary care hospital, new systems must be designed that allow the nurse to travel to the patient's environment. Further, systems must provide community-based nurses with timely access to comprehensive and useable information for planning, coordinating, and evaluating patient care.

The Omaha system has been used as a taxonomy on which to build assessment and care planning (Martin and Scheet 1992). The Omaha system and other data management tools have helped nursing staff and administration to shift from a process-driven to a data-driven paradigm. Nurses also have been able to use structured information as a focal point for dialogue with patients, physicians, and other nurses. From a research standpoint, the taxonomy has allowed for meaningful data queries and has been sensitive to statistical manipulation.

Several functions must be considered when designing clinical information systems. Specific requirements depend on the setting, patient population, and provider mix. Some important system capabilities include the following (Zielstorff et al. 1993):

- *Acquiring:* The system must be able to capture all patient data needed for patient care.
- *Structuring:* Patient and population data should be structured with accepted vocabularies and classification systems.
- *Timing:* The system must be able to capture all data generated in the course of patient care as close to the time and place of creation as possible and in the most efficient manner possible.
- *Storing:* Patient-specific data should be stored and secured independently of the programs that collect the data.
- *Reporting:* Data elements should be constructed in a manner such that they can serve multiple users and multiple purposes.
- *Indexing:* Unlimited keys for indexing the data should be allowed.
- *Transforming:* The system should be capable of transforming data to information and information to knowledge.
- *Mapping:* The system should be capable of mapping to and from various constructs and vocabularies.
- *Presenting:* The system should accommodate the level of expertise of the practitioner.
- *Facilitating:* Data, information, and knowledge should be presented in the format most suitable to assist decision making.
- *Questioning:* The system should be able to tailor queries of the data to various disciplines and should support ad hoc queries from end users.

Information systems have become integral components of nursing educational curricula, professional practice, and research agendas (National Center for Nursing Research 1993; Zielstorff et al.1993; Werley et al. 1991; Ryan and Delaney 1995). Nursing informatics and the dynamics of the health care revolution offer new career opportunities for nurses (Simpson 1992 and 1993).

The phenomenal expansion of clinical information available, the complexity of needs in at-risk populations, and health care redesign issues have had a profound impact on nursing. For instance, nurses are called on to make sound clinical decisions in the field with little opportunity for face-to-face contact with professionals or other information sources. Nurses must be integrally involved in the design of information systems in order to advance the discipline of nursing.

In addition to information systems, other exciting inroads have been made in nursing involvement in the design, use, and evaluation of clinical information technologies. Currently, for example, a research team, including the Visiting Nurses Association of Greater Philadelphia, Tevital, Inc., and The Pennsylvania State University, is exploring the use of in-home computer devices in helping home health nurses and diabetic patients to manage their illness. The study is testing an innovative technology that combines interactive voice, video, and clinical data using ordinary telephone lines to facilitate communication between patients and home health nurses. Outcomes under study include the impact on general health status, quality of life, costs associated with home health care, patient satisfaction, and the extension of this technology to other populations (Dansky 1997).

The use of information systems and clinical technology is not limited to one discipline. All health care professions are confronting the need for knowledge and skills in information technologies. Additionally, providing language systems that capture the richness of each discipline, yet are understandable and generalizable to professionals from other disciplines, is a serious challenge. Growth in this area has been influenced by an exploding knowledge base, emerging technologies, consumer and payer expectations of quality, and evolving standards of care.

Role of Information in Clinical Decision Making

Today's health care environment provides a paradox for clinical and administrative decision makers. On one hand, the health care delivery system is rich with technology, personnel, and the availability of information. On the other hand, integrating these elements into comprehensible and meaningful decision-making resources presents a huge challenge for clinicians, particularly given the complexity of patient-care problems. The issue of confidentiality must be addressed. These difficulties are compounded by the move from decisions based on individual patients to those based on population-based care strategies.

Decision-Making Framework

Risk taking in clinical decision making must involve informed choices. The following discussion provides a framework for identifying, analyzing, and comparing risks and information with the goal of sound decision making (Eddy 1990). Health care is governed by decisions centered around the questions of what to do, how to do it, and when to do it. The unifying goal of clinical decision making is to choose the action that is most likely to result in the outcome the patient wants.

The first step is to identify all the possible clinical treatment options and their associated outcomes. This step involves collecting all available evidence regarding costs, benefits, side effects, and outcomes of each option, and it requires synthesizing pertinent research as well as integrating clinical expertise and experience. Although this step primarily is based on facts, it also involves subjective judgments to a degree (Eddy 1990).

The next step is more a question of personal preferences and values. It involves weighing the benefits and harms, balancing outcomes and costs, and giving priority to the option with the highest yield to the cost. Costs include emotional energy (e.g., anxiety prior to a procedure), time, financial, and other quality-of-life issues. The patient is essential in this step, and it is patient preferences that guide this part of the process (Eddy 1990).

Decision-Making Pitfalls

Flaws in decision making can occur at either of two junctures. The information about outcomes of a decision may be wrong or misperceived, or the value patients place on the outcomes may be misconstrued. In the first case, important information about outcomes may be incomplete, ignored, misinterpreted, or exaggerated. In the second, misperceptions about patient preferences

may occur. Patients may not understand an outcome or the explanation of its effectiveness. Patients may not be consulted at all, or physicians may project their own preferences on the process (Eddy 1990).

Role of Information in Financial Aspects of Care

Clinical decision making is one reason for the use of information systems. In managed care, clinical aspects and financial dimensions are linked. Therefore, information systems must provide a dialogue from both clinical and financial perspectives.

Financial risk provides the imperative for MCOs to closely track health costs and utilization patterns. Information systems provide a mechanism for MCOs to compare budgeted with actual performance at the organizational level. Typically, MCOs use information to evaluate practice patterns, calculate incentive payments, and reward or modify provider behavior (Grimaldi 1995).

Financial information systems are generally structured to yield pertinent information about patient mix and service utilization. Grimaldi (1995) has categorized performance measures into six general types used to evaluate provider cost and utilization patterns. Each of these measures represents an average and can be calculated monthly, quarterly, or annually:

1. *Cost per unit of service:* Total amount paid for a particular service divided by the total number of units provided; for example, the total amount paid for home health nursing visits divided by total number of visits. This measure reflects an average cost over a specified time period.
2. *Cost of service PMPM:* Total amount spent for a service divided by the total number of member months. The number of member months is the sum of the number of months each member is enrolled during the time period.
3. *Cost of service per user:* Amount spent for a particular service divided by the number of members who received it. This allows the evaluation of the amount spent on services for users as distinct from all members.

4. *Units of service PMPM:* Amount reflects the total units of service divided by the total number of member months.

5. *Units of service per user:* Total units of service divided by the number of members who received that service.

6. *Units of service per 1,000 members:* Total units divided by the total number of member months and then multiplied by 12,000. The average reflects the annualized use of service by 1,000 members each enrolled for 12 continuous months.

Types of Data Reports to Support Managed Clinical Care

The quality of clinical decision making depends on the information guiding the decisions. Sound clinical judgments require accurate and timely information. This concept is not new; Florence Nightingale developed and relied on patient status reports in the 1800s. Information allows the movement from focusing on only one patient to expanding care for groups and populations.

The following examples are provided as a bridge from individual patient care to a clinical scope that includes caring for groups or populations of patients. The tools summarize information about individuals and groups. They are not designed to replace clinical judgment, but rather to enhance it.

Individual Patient Reports

Individual patient reports are generated from information provided by the patient. As with any patient information, confidentiality must be protected. The reports are designed to give the clinician a quick sketch of the patient's demographics, health status, risk triggers, preventive health information, functional status, and service use. This information is used as a baseline estimate of what other information will be needed depending on how at-risk the patient is. By looking through individual patient reports, nurses can triage patients into categories, then plan and provide care based on the priorities that come from this information. Of course, clinic charts, provider feedback, and consultations with other team members also may reveal factors that influence decisions. It is important to document these, so that a decision trail is left for others who might need to follow up.

Provider Reports

Provider reports are the first step in team planning for population-based care. Provider reports organize and summarize grouped (aggregated) patient information so that teams can plan according to their panels. The provider reports are organized by primary care provider, so clinicians can get a summary of their panels regarding enrollment date, gender, age, general health, number of health conditions, number of prescription medications, functional status, service use, and trigger scores. This information also can be used to draw comparisons between panels.

Reports of this kind have many uses. Information can be used to mark changes in a panel's health, functional status, service use, and risk over time. Providers can access information on patients by clinical parameters. For instance, nurse practitioners can find out how many diabetic patients are on their panel and sort them by prescribed medications or demographics.

The ability to ask questions of clinical information provides clinicians with another tool to strengthen clinical decision making. Information can be used to formulate population-based strategies and evaluate progress toward goals. The information can be used to guide staffing and planning decisions. Perhaps most important, it can be used by provider teams to self-evaluate their care at the population level. This concept is relatively new in health care, and one that requires much further development.

These types of individual patient reports and provider reports represent innovative ways of informing care for individuals and groups. If health care professionals screen for risk, then use the information to provide the appropriate level and intensity of care, patients receive high quality health care that is not duplicative or lacking. A focus on populations will allow health care teams to allocate health care resources in a responsible, evidence-based manner.

Implications for Nursing

Information systems hold vast potential in terms of clinical and financial management of MCOs. Nursing leadership can play a pivotal role in guiding the development of information systems and their application. Creation of an effective decision-making environment requires a nurturing of the willingness to take risks, make choices, and contribute to goal attainment. Effective leadership promotes excellence by supporting clinicians in their decision making in a way that results in actions and changes that move toward a goal. Leadership also must provide the value system within which decisions can be made, actions guided, and evaluations formulated. Encouragement and support of decision making is critical. Research has revealed the following essential elements that support the logic of decision making (Larson and LaFasto 1989):

- To achieve a new goal or vision, change must take place.
- For change to happen, a decision must be made.
- To make a choice, a risk must be taken.
- To encourage risk taking, a supportive climate must exist.

- Organizational leadership must provide resources for decision making.

Nurses who are knowledgeable in financial, clinical, and informational aspects of managed care will have many exciting career opportunities. Nursing informatics pertains to theories and processes of clinical reasoning and the management of uncertainty in clinical practice. Nursing informatics, coupled with clinical and financial knowledge, will allow clinicians, administrators, researchers, educators, and policymakers to influence the health care arena in a positive and powerful way.

Information, clinical care, and financial indicators are linked in a new way in managed care. When used in combination to the best of their potential, these components provide clinicians and patients with tools to achieve better integrated, high quality care. Nursing has a responsibility to ensure the confidentiality of patient information within the emerging systems. The essential link that information systems provide is a way to track outcomes linked to specific patients, provider panels, and patient populations.

8

Outcomes Management

CHAPTER OBJECTIVES

- Describe the current emphasis on outcomes in health care.
- Outline major contributions from medicine and nursing related to outcomes definition and measurement.
- Describe outcomes measurement and management from a managed care perspective.
- Highlight implications for nursing.

Traditionally, the emphasis of health care research and evaluation was predominantly on structures and processes of care. Structures included such measures as hospital beds, technologies available, and numbers of providers. Process measures included variables such as morbidity and mortality rates and rates of procedures and surgeries. Not only did research focus on these aspects of health care, but also did standards for accreditation and regulation.

Recently, the focus has broadened to encompass the exploration and documentation of outcomes, especially from the patient's perspective (Tarlov et al. 1989, Kelly et al. 1994). Consumers, payers, and providers want evidence that treatments work. The emphasis on patient outcomes has resulted in member satisfaction questionnaires, consumer report cards, and published health plan ratings (Cook and Nolan 1996).

Efforts toward measuring and documenting outcomes have been influenced by policy, payment mechanisms, and changing societal values (Wright 1993). There has been a paradigm shift from one that values expert opinion of a single provider to a new framework founded on evidence-based information. The major issues include cost, quality, and access to care. MCOs rely on outcomes information such as performance data in order to provide high quality and to contain costs.

Many of the outcomes studies conducted to date focus on care provided by a particular discipline or for a particular illness. Although this work provides a strong foundation, future outcomes initiatives must examine the interdependence of health care providers. In addition, the clinical and financial outcomes associated with patient care must be recognized in order to address current problems with the health care system.

Multidisciplinary Approach

Efforts to evaluate patient outcomes are emerging from several health-related disciplines. This section concentrates on outcomes research in medicine and nursing because these two paths of research converge clinically, conceptually, and operationally. Patients do not present with problems that can be neatly defined as "medical" or "nursing" in nature; health problems and their causes cross traditional disciplinary lines (Leath and Thatcher 1991).

Medicine and nursing approach patient care from two distinct perspectives. Medicine has a primary responsibility to diagnose and treat disease processes, whereas nursing emphasizes the patients' life experiences and response to alterations in health (Bates 1970, Kalisch and Kalisch 1980). Collaborative teamwork between medicine and nursing is a viable way to address health care delivery and have an impact on patient outcomes (Schraeder, Britt, and Shelton 1995; Shelton et al. 1994; Cramer and Tucker 1995). Because each health care provider who works with a patient contributes to that patient's outcome, evaluating quality and cost requires assessing the effectiveness of all interventions, not just those based on physicians' prescriptions (Kelly et al. 1994).

The inclusion of collaborative efforts between medicine and nursing in research on measurement of patient outcomes is critical in the current health care environment. First, the inroads that medicine and nursing have made will be considered. Then the role of outcomes measurement in managed care will be explored.

Medical Outcomes Study

The Medical Outcomes Study (MOS) has been recognized as a seminal effort in measuring patient outcomes using instruments that are both practical and valid (Tarlov et al. 1989). The conceptual framework for the MOS represents an expanded view of medical research because of its focus on patient perceptions of health and well-being and the endeavor to investigate implications of medical care from the patients' perspective. The two-year observational research study was conducted at multiple sites in the United States and was designed to examine key aspects of physician care that are associated with favorable patient outcomes. Both cross-sectional and longitudinal data were collected (Tarlov et al. 1989).

The conceptual framework for the MOS included variables corresponding to the structure and process of physician care and patient outcomes. This represented three major departures from prior medical research:

- Patient perceptions were sought and quantified;
- Physician researchers were evaluating care of other physicians; and
- Outcomes of care were measured, quantified, and emphasized in the analysis.

The MOS was organized around Donabedian's paradigm for evaluation using three components of quality: structure, process, and outcomes (Donabedian 1968). The conceptual framework expanded on traditional ways of measuring structures and processes of care and was a forerunner of much of the emerging research on quality. Structure included descriptors of the health system characteristics unique to the institution or setting (organizational structure, specialty mix, financial incentives, workload, and access to and convenience of care for patients); provider demographics and characteristics; and patient demographics, health habits, beliefs, and preferences. Process of care included technical style (number of visits, medications, referrals, tests, hospitalizations, expenditures, and continuity and coordination of care) and interpersonal style (patient participation, counseling, and communication level) (Tarlov et al. 1989).

In addition to structures and processes, the model measured four categories of outcomes: clinical end points, functional status, general well-being, and satisfaction with care. The MOS focused on five chronic conditions: hypertension, recent myocardial infarction, congestive heart failure, diabetes, and depression. Many reports by the MOS researchers are emerging in the literature, and results continue to shape health care policy and delivery modalities.

Although it represents a major and enduring contribution to the understanding of patient-focused outcomes of medical care, the MOS does not address certain key variables. Serious limitations of the MOS include measurement of the impact of only one provider (physician) on patient outcomes and omission of cost as an outcome in the model. Modifications to the framework have been suggested (Kelly et al. 1994), including delineating other provider-specific intervention domains, such as nursing. In addition, incorporating multidisciplinary provider influences on patient outcomes and including the outcome of cost would strengthen the framework (Kelly et al. 1994).

Outcomes Research in Nursing

In a comprehensive review of the literature on outcomes measurement in nursing, Marek (1989) noted the pioneering efforts of Florence Nightingale in using mortality data to convey the need for improved standards of care during the Crimean War (Nightingale 1858). Marek described trends in nursing research and policy efforts aimed at improving and measuring quality outcomes. Historically, outcomes have been used to examine the impact of staffing and education issues (Adelotte 1962), to document and measure quality (Joint Commission on Accreditation of Hospitals 1975), and for local nursing audits (Hover and Zimmer 1978, Decker 1979). The mid-1980s witnessed a resurgence in the use of outcome criteria to evaluate care, largely due to sociopolitical changes and the emphasis on payment mechanisms such as prospective payment and Medicare and Medicaid programs (Lohr 1988; Joint Commission on Accreditation of Healthcare Organizations 1987; Roper et al. 1988). Long-term care and home health care became more outcome-focused as well (Hannon, O'Donald, and Lefkowich 1984; Lefkowich, 1985; Grimaldi, Micheletti, and Shala 1987; Rinke 1988).

More recently, accomplishments have been made in establishing uniform standards for the collection and categorization of minimum essential nursing data, the Nursing Minimum Data Set (NMDS) (Werley and Lang 1988, 402–411). A research group at the University of Iowa provided a rich source of describing and classifying nursing interventions (Nursing Intervention Classification, NIC) (Bulechek and McCloskey 1990, 3–28; McCloskey and Bulechek 1992). Research highlighting the outcomes of nursing interventions based on the Omaha system (Martin and Scheet 1992) has been reported in the literature (Martin, Scheet, and Stegman 1993, Martin, Leak, and Aden 1992). Currently, a research team at the University of Iowa is conducting a major study to identify and classify nursing-sensitive patient outcomes (Kraus 1994).

Marek's definition of outcome is "a measurable change in a client's health status related to the receipt of nursing care" (1989, 3). Marek developed a typology of nursing outcome indicators, which includes physiological, psychosocial, functional, behavioral, cognitive, symptomatic, satisfaction, well-being, home maintenance, goal attainment, use of resources, safety, and resolution of nursing diagnoses or problems (Marek 1989). These indicators are similar to those featured in the Medical Outcomes Study as outcomes of physician care, yet they reflect the nursing perspective. The challenge is to build upon the research on patient care outcomes to date by developing a multidisciplinary model that includes a patient-centered approach and measures clinical end points, functional status, general well-being, satisfaction with care, and cost (Marek 1989; Kelly et al. 1994; Tarlov et al. 1989).

Outcomes Measurement in Managed Care

Managed care offers a variety of organizational conditions that enhance the capability to measure, monitor, and manage outcomes. In addition to financial incentives to monitor outcomes, MCOs have structural aspects that make outcome studies more feasible than in fee-for-service care. For example, because patients are linked to a primary care provider who must provide or authorize all services, clinical care is easier to track than if patients self-refer to several providers. In addition, since payment is linked to patient-provider encounters, information systems are usually in place that allow clinical care and charges to be traced. Also, reports can be given to individual providers containing outcomes and feedback specific to their patient panels. These three aspects of managed care provide significant advantages in terms of exploring which services were provided to a population, subpopulations, and individuals. This information is a rich resource when it comes to planning and evaluating services.

MCOs have the potential to systematically identify individuals with specific diseases or risk factors and to improve outcomes. To realize this potential, MCOs require specific tools and resources, including information systems that support identification and triage of members into risk groups and subsequent administration of care targeted to risk status (O'Connor, Rush, and Pronk 1997).

Health care providers are faced with the challenge of proving the value of the services they deliver. MCOs must be able to track costs and outcomes for all their patients in order to demonstrate value for dollars spent on health care. Patients also are demanding information about outcomes as they become more knowledgeable about disease and treatment modalities (Ortmeier 1997). As Bower (1996) noted, "Outcomes have long been important to health care providers and institutions, and the current environment is making them critical" (excerpted with permission of the publisher).

Many factors have influenced the increased interest in outcomes measurement, reporting, and management. The financial incentives in managed care have certainly helped establish the need for well-articulated, easily measured, meaningful outcome studies. Capitation, in order to be successful, must focus on payment of treatment strategies that are effective clinically and financially. Measuring outcomes is one way of investigating the value and quality of treatment processes in terms of clinical outcomes.

Many MCOs are measuring outcomes in order to judge where they are in terms of their competition. For instance, if an MCO is experiencing a higher rate of infection after cardiac surgery, it spends more to provide adequate care in the long term. Also, employer groups would potentially be less interested in purchasing managed care coverage if it is known to be of poor quality. In this way, care delivery and financing are again linked in terms of outcomes management.

Whereas outcomes information is useful in financial planning and formulating market strategies, outcomes measurement also plays an integral role in accreditation of MCOs. For instance, since 1997, HMOs with Medicare risk contracts have been required to submit an outcomes report based on HEDIS (Health Plan Employer Data and Information Set) criteria. HMOs will obtain most reporting information from encounter databases and clinical records and will follow reporting guidelines established by the National Committee for Quality Assurance (NCQA) (Grimaldi 1997). HEDIS 3.0 contains multiple measures regarding effectiveness of care, access/availability of care, satisfaction with the experience of care, health plan stability, use of services, cost of care, informed care choices, and health plan descriptive information (NCQA 1996).

Selecting Outcomes Measurement Tools

Several considerations must be taken into account when selecting outcomes and tools for measurement. Many instruments have been designed that capture and measure different aspects of health, including social, biological, general, and disease-specific dimensions (Greenfield and Nelson 1992, Schraeder, Shelton, Britt, Parker, and Leonard 1997). Selection of instruments is based on several criteria, including the following (Radosevich 1997):

- *Sensibility:* Does the measure tap clinically and socially important dimensions of health? Does it fit the purpose and framework of the intervention, program, or organization?
- *Comprehensible output:* Can the measure be interpreted and understood?
- *Content validity:* Does the measure have clinical significance and universal application?
- *Reliability:* Does the measure provide consistent values between patients?
- *Validity:* Does the measure accurately predict an outcome?
- *Responsiveness:* Does the measure have the power to detect clinically and socially important differences?
- *Burden:* How much does administering the measure cost in terms of time and money?
- *Scoring:* Can the measure be easily and accurately scored?

Selecting the most useful measures for outcomes studies is important, but there are other critical processes. The following steps have been identified in developing an outcomes program (Ortmeier 1997):

- Identify the disease or condition to be studied.
- Identify patient demographics and comorbidities.
- Identify current treatment and intervention options.
- Identify health care resource utilization for affected patient populations.
- Assign system-specific costs to resource utilization for each treatment alternative.
- Identify outcomes to be measured.
- Identify interventions to optimize patient care.
- Assess baseline resource utilization.
- Implement intervention program.
- Evaluate outcomes.
- Review and evaluate program effectiveness.
- Alter program intervention on the basis of effectiveness.

Implications for Nursing

Historians tracing the roots of outcomes studies and investigations on quality frequently point to Florence Nightingale's work in documenting patient outcomes in the Crimean War as a pioneering venture in this area (Lohr and Brook 1984). The discipline of nursing has a tradition of planning care with goals and objectives (re: outcomes) in mind. Measuring and evaluating progress is a key element in the nursing process. The new challenge for nursing is to expand the focus from patient-specific care to population-based planning and outcomes management.

The emphasis on outcomes derives from several trends in health care, not the least of which is that patients have become consumers and health care has become a more competitive enterprise. Likewise, information about the value of health care products and services has become more readily available as computer technology and research methodologies have grown more sophisticated.

Outcomes measurement and research has the goal of evaluating how types and costs of health care affect patient care, well-being, and health status (Lewis 1995). However, data collection must not be the end of the process. Ultimately, the collection of information about outcomes should lead to analysis and recommendations for improving care modalities. Nurses can be a vital link in interpreting outcomes information and translating new information into revolutionary health practices.

Outcomes measurement leads to outcomes management. Outcomes management is "a process for defining, reviewing, assimilating, and evaluating the health care that is delivered to clients" [Flarey 1996 (excerpted with permission of the publisher)]. It is the use of specific outcomes to shape and evaluate care in a continuous manner. Nurses can play vital roles in this process if they are knowledgeable about health care provision, financing, and information management.

Case Study: Roles for Nursing and the Community Nursing Organization

9

To illustrate possible roles and systems of nursing care that use managed care structures, this chapter presents a case study on the Community Nursing Organization (CNO), a federally funded demonstration investigating innovative nursing roles and financing structures. The CNO model, which was designed to provide specific health care services to Medicare beneficiaries via a nurse-managed delivery system under capitated financing, is described in this case study.

A perplexing situation in health care today is the delivery and financing of services for the elderly. Clearly, this is an example of the challenges spurring widespread exploration of alternative ways of providing health care to the population. This highlights the need for new health care strategies to coordinate, finance, and provide services to the elderly. Delivery models must be developed to provide a complete spectrum of managed care to achieve a realistic balance between the elderly's level of medical need, functional status, individual health preference, and cost.

Overview

The CNO is a five-year national demonstration, established by Congress in the Omnibus Budget Reconciliation Act of 1987, Section 4079. Agencies that helped in drafting the legislation included the American Nurses Association (ANA) and the People-to-People Health Foundation (Project HOPE). This legislation enabled the Health Care Financing Administration (HCFA) to conduct demonstration projects to test prepaid, capitated payments for community nursing and ambulatory care services provided to Medicare beneficiaries. Capitation strives to replace multiple payment mechanisms with the use of tools such as reasonable cost, predetermined fee schedules, and usual, customary, and prevailing costs.

The purpose of the CNO is to provide specified, coordinated, cost-effective health care services in non-institutional settings to the elderly. This reflects several goals and principles valued by health policymakers: (1) prevention of unnecessary institutionalization through health promotion, maintenance, and restorative nursing care; (2) continuity across the care spectrum; (3) choice of health care providers; (4) use of prospective payment mechanisms; (5) encouragement of competitive pricing of services; (6) adherence to capitation payment; and (7) provision of quality nursing and ambulatory care services.

Goals and objectives for the CNO include (1) examination of the types of organizations, organizational frameworks, and approaches used to carry out the CNO model; (2) assessment of the operational and financial viability of the model under a capitated payment system; and (3) evaluation of the effects of the CNO on the access, continuity, and quality of care of Medicare expenditures.

Four national sites were selected to participate: Carondelet Health Care, Tucson, Arizona (Etheridge and Lamb 1989, Michaels 1991); Carle Clinic Association, Urbana, Illinois (Schraeder, Lamb, Shelton, and Britt 1997, Shelton et al. 1994); Visiting Nurse Service (VNS) of New York, New York (Denker 1993); and Living at Home/Block Nurse Program (LAH/BNP), St. Paul, Minnesota (Jamieson 1990). The sites represent diverse geographic and cultural areas and organizational structures. Each of the four sites has strong community-based nursing programs. Carondelet, LAH/BNP, and VNS have been designated as urban sites, and Carle Clinic is the one rural site.

A key component of the CNO delivery model is the role of the primary nurse provider (PNP). The PNP's role is to determine, with the patient or family, the appropriate mix, duration, intensity, and timing of health services. The role of the PNP is, at times, similar to the role of a home health care nurse in a capitated HMO setting, with the additional responsibilities associated with the conduct of research and the accountability of service authorization. The PNP authorizes payment for CNO-covered services, and may also coordinate (but not pay for) non-covered services if the situation warrants. The PNP's assessment, education, monitoring, and case management functions are involved in all demonstration services. The CNO uses capitated payment and PNP skills as mechanisms to increase access to needed services and promote more timely and appropriate use of community health services.

Administrative Structure and Case Management Functions

Nursing occupies the central role in administration of the CNO. Although the sites have different organizational structures, they share common characteristics in the delivery of nurse-managed health services. Nursing involvement encompasses management and administrative functions, assessment, service authorization and coordination, and case management. All project directors are registered nurses (RNs) who have responsibility for oversight of all management and administrative functions and coordination with HCFA and evaluators.

Membership Eligibility

To be eligible for membership in the CNO, potential enrollees must meet the following requirements: (1) live in the defined catchment area of one of the four CNO sites; (2) maintain active status in Medicare Part A and B; (3) obtain all CNO-covered services, except in emergencies, from the CNO; and (4) not have a diagnosis with end stage renal disease or be enrolled in hospice or in a risk contract HMO.

Enrollment and Assessment Process

Medicare beneficiaries must go through several steps before they become CNO members. Once potential enrollees have been identified, they must meet the enrollment criteria outlined previously. Subsequently, potential enrollees participate in an initial face-to-face interview. During the interview, several types of data are collected, including demographics, functional status, health perception, and previous use of and satisfaction with health services. After the initial baseline interview, all individuals are randomized into either the control or treatment group. Individuals randomized into the treatment group participate in an in-depth nursing assessment based on the Omaha system of patient problem identification (Martin and Scheet 1992) and care planning. Members prioritize problems and identify intervention strategies with their PNP. After the nursing assessment and written care plan are completed, CNO members are eligible for covered services. Assessments and care plans are updated in face-to-face interviews every six months and as needed.

Although control group members do not receive CNO services, their Medicare claims and health status provide comparison data with the treatment group in order to measure effects of the CNO on patient care and health care costs. The health status of control group members is monitored every 12 months.

Primary Nurse Providers

PNPs are responsible for the administrative coordination of health services for CNO enrollees. They also collect research data, conduct comprehensive assessments, facilitate care planning, authorize services for appropriate levels of care, and undertake other case management functions. PNPs may provide direct physical care as well.

PNPs complete comprehensive assessments in the office and in the home, if necessary, for each enrollee. The assessment process allows for mutual identification of problems and the formulation of care plans, which specify interventions by formal and informal providers. Formal services include CNO services authorized by the PNP. Informal services include assistance provided by the enrollee, family, friends, neighbors, and community. Enrollee agreements are completed and signed by the PNP and the enrollee, signifying mutual agreement with the care plan.

PNPs have a direct role in the fiscal operations of the CNO. They are responsible for the authorization of and payment for capitated CNO services. Because services are approved and paid for by the CNO, PNPs have unique leverage concerning the monitoring of service units and costs from both enrollee and provider perspectives. The PNP manager supervises CNO operations and oversees all authorizations. PNPs may authorize home care services, in which case they coordinate with the direct care RN and the RN supervisor to establish the plan of care within the capitation framework. In addition to the PNP service, CNO-covered services include outpatient ambulatory care services usually covered under traditional Medicare.

A major benefit of CNO participation is the involvement of the PNP in assessment and case management. It was estimated by the CNO sites that approximately 20 percent of all enrollees would use or be at risk for using CNO-covered services. This percentage is relatively large for a capitated system and it is management of this segment that represents the main source of financial risk for the CNO and the major opportunity to test the cost-effectiveness of the model. Thus, the case management component has two primary purposes. One is managing and providing care to enrollees with chronic or acute conditions; the other is reducing health risk for enrollees through activities aimed at teaching, monitoring, and supporting health promotion and disease prevention. Capitation provides strong financial incentives for preventing unnecessary and inappropriate use of health services.

Capitation System

The CNO is reimbursed on a PMPM basis by HCFA. The CNOs receive a fixed monthly payment for each enrollee, based on age, gender, and number of home health care visits in the past six months. For three of the four CNO sites, each member's functional status also is factored into the monthly capitation rate.

Evaluation

The CNO evaluation is attempting to measure the impact of capitated, community-based nursing care, enrollee-centered decision making, and coordination of services on enrollees' health status and service utilization. The evaluation is designed to test the following hypotheses relative to differences between treatment and control conditions: (1) use of CNO-covered services will be lower; (2) use of hospital and physician services will be similar, or lower; (3) non-Medicare-covered community services will be used more intensively; (4) functional status scores will be higher; and (5) health problem ratings will show improvement or resolution.

The CNO evaluation also includes qualitative measures. Periodic interviews have been conducted with CNO staff, sponsoring organizations, service providers, community organizations, and CNO enrollees throughout the three years of the demonstration to gather information on a number of issues related to the demonstration. The CNO represents new directions and innovative roles nurses can play in the evolving health care system. At the time of this writing the four CNO sites were awaiting the final evaluation report, which should be distributed by HCFA in late 1998 or early 1999.

10

Summary

The health care system is experiencing increased complexity and vast changes. This dynamic environment is accompanied by an increased diversity of providers competing for the opportunity to deliver services. Prospective payment, new technologies, health maintenance strategies, and capitated financing mechanisms have changed the face of health care delivery. The current focus of health care is on quality improvement: gathering information, identifying performance objectives and variances, and improving care with structured care models (Weiss 1997). New financial mechanisms and contractual arrangements have been created to meet these changes in the delivery of care. MCOs are an integral component in the restructuring of health care.

Managed care has presented the health care system with complex challenges. The intricate relationships between the delivery and financing of care within managed care structures has changed the way consumers and professionals perceive health care. Social and political controversies about managed care have emerged, yet the benefits and disadvantages of the system have not been well defined. The dynamic delivery system, social values inherent in health care, multiple ways managed care is operationalized, and the perplexing array of strategic alliances among plans, providers, and employer groups have contributed to the current environment.

Nursing faces its own unique set of demands within this complicated and ever-changing environment. The traditional emphasis on purely clinical aspects of care is being replaced by a perspective that highlights individual patient care, but pragmatically takes into account financial factors as well. The challenge is to prevent the focus on patient care from being diluted by financial constraints while still developing a realistic sense of what care is responsibly administered. This potential tension between clinical and financial priorities is an area in which nursing involvement can greatly benefit patients.

Most nursing roles have traditionally been somewhat isolated from the financial aspects of care delivery. As a profession, nursing must become more literate, informed, and involved in the financial considerations of health care. It is within this new context that nursing informatics, population-focused care, outcomes management, evidence-based care, and guidelines can be incorporated into integrated systems of care delivery.

What does the future hold for managed care? For nursing roles within managed care? A proactive stance is needed in order for nursing to shape delivery models that offer the best care for patients. Yet it is difficult to be proactive in a system as complex and changeable as our health care system has been in the past 20 years. An environment of competition and rapid transitions, mergers, acquisitions, and downsizing provides the context for this debate. It will be critical for the nursing profession to demonstrate its value in solving the issues that emerge. This will require continued efforts in education, research, collaboration, policy development, and clinical excellence.

This monograph has provided basic definitions for typical aspects of managed care delivery and financing systems. It has explored population-based care strategies such as risk screening, demand management, case management, and patient self-management. It has offered a brief overview of risk models and an outline of utilization management. Information management and outcomes measurement in nursing have been discussed because of their vast potential to help nursing shape the future of health care delivery. Finally, a case study of the Community Nursing Organization has been included to provide examples of nursing roles in managed care.

References

Adelotte, M. 1962. The Use of Patient Welfare as a Criterion Measure. *Nursing Research* 11(1): 10–14.

Aliotta, S. 1996. Components of a Successful Case Management Program. In *Managed Care and Chronic Illness.* Edited by P. Fox and T. Fama. Gaithersburg, Md.: Aspen Publishers, Inc.

Amos, L. K., and J. R. Graves. 1989. Knowledge Technology: Costs, Benefits, and Ethical Considerations. In *Current Issues in Nursing,* 3d edition. Edited by J. McClosky and E. Grace. Boston: Blackwell Scientific.

Azzahir, M., J. Grant-Shambaugh, R. Jeddeloh, K. Juliar, and P. Schaefer. 1995. "Healthier Communities: Why All the Fuss?" Presented at The Healthcare Quest: Creativity in Capitation, Minneapolis, Minn., July 15–16.

Bates, B. 1970. Doctor and Nurse: Changing Roles and Relations. *New England Journal of Medicine* 283: 129.

Blendon, R., M. Brodie, J. Benson, D. Altman, L. Levitt, T. Hoff, and L. Hugick. 1998. Understanding the Managed Care Backlash. *Health Affairs* 17: 80–94.

Bodenheimer, T., and K. Grumbach. 1996. Capitation or Decapitation: Keeping Your Head in Changing Times. *Journal of the American Medical Association* 276(13): 1025–1031.

Bower, K. 1996. Outcomes and Their Management. *Seminars for Nurse Managers: Strategies for Leadership and Management* 4: 147–150.

Britt, T. 1998. Managed Care and Managing Risks. In *Take Control: A Guide to Risk Management.* Edited by L. Shinn. Kirke-Van Orsdel, Inc.

Bulechek, G. M., and J. C. McCloskey. 1990. Nursing Intervention Taxonomy Development. In *Current Issues in Nursing.* Edited by J. C. McClosky and H. K. Grace. St. Louis, Mo.: C.V. Mosby.

Case Management Society of America. 1995. *Standards of Practice for Case Management.* Little Rock: CMSA.

Christianson, J., R. Taylor, and D. Knutson. 1998. *Restructuring Chronic Illness Management.* San Francisco: Jossey–Bass Publishers.

Clouten, K., and R. Weber. 1994. Patient-Focused Care . . . Playing to Win. *Nursing Management* 25: 34–36.

Cohen, E., and T. Cesta. 1997. *Nursing Case Management: From Concept to Evaluation,* 2d edition. St. Louis: Mosby.

Cook, T., and W. Nolan. 1996. A Nurse Practitioner-Led, Collaborative, Outpatient Practice: A Case Study in Outcomes Management. *Seminars for Nurse Managers: Strategies for Leadership and Management* 4: 154–162.

Cramer, D., and S. M. Tucker. 1995. The Consumer's Role in Quality: Partnering for Quality Outcomes. *Journal of Nursing Care Quality* 9(2): 54–66.

Daly, B. 1997. Acute Care Nurse Practitioners: "Strangers in a Strange Land." *AACN Clinical Issues* 8(1): 93–100.

Dansky, K. 1997. *Use of Telehealth to Improve Home Health Services.* Grant proposal funded under United States General Accounting Office: Telemedicine: Federal Strategy is Needed to Guide Investments. GAO/NSIAD/HEHS-97-76.

Decker, F. 1979. Using Patient Outcomes to Evaluate Community Health Nursing. *Nursing Outlook* 27: 278–282.

Denker, E. 1993. *Healing at Home: Visiting Nurse Service of New York, 1893–1993.* New York: Visiting Nurse Service of New York.

Donabedian, A. 1968. Promoting Quality Through Evaluation: The Process of Patient Care. *Medical Care* 6: 181–202.

Eddy, D. 1990. Clinical Decision Making: From Theory to Practice. *Journal of the American Medical Association* 263: 287–290.

Eddy, D., and J. Malcolm. 1995. "Checking on the Community." Presented at The Healthcare Quest: Creativity in Capitation, Minneapolis, Minn., July 15–16.

Etheridge, P., and G. Lamb. 1989. Professional Nursing Case Management Improves Quality, Access, and Costs. *Nursing Management* 20: 26–29.

Flarey, D. 1996. Outcomes Management: A Primer for Nurse Managers. *Seminars for Nurse Managers: Strategies for Leadership and Management* 4: 139–141.

Graff, W., W. Bensussen-Walls, E. Cody, and J. Williamson. 1995. Population Management in an HMO: New Rules for Nursing. *Public Health Nursing* 12: 213–221.

Graves, J. R., and S. Corcoran. 1989. The Study of Nursing Informatics. *Image: The Journal of Nursing Scholarship* 21: 227–231.

Greenfield, S., and E. Nelson. 1992. Recent Developments and Future Issues in the Use of Health Assessment Measures in Clinical Settings. *Medical Care (Suppl.)* MS23–MS41.

Grimaldi, P. 1997. HMOs Must Submit Medicare HEDIS. *Nursing Management* 28: 54–55.

Grimaldi, P. 1996. Manage Authorizations to Manage Care. *Nursing Management* 27(4): 49–51.

Grimaldi, P. 1995. Capitation Savvy a Must. *Nursing Management* 26: 33–34.

Grimaldi, P. L., J. A. Micheletti, and T. J. Shala. 1987. Quality Assurance in a Cost and Case-Mix Environment. *Quality Review Bulletin* 13(5): 170–174.

Hannon, E. L., J. F. O'Donald, and W. K. Lefkowich. 1984. The Restructuring and Evaluation of the Patient Medical Review in New York State. *Journal of Long Term Care Administration* 12(2): 10–18.

Holman, H., and K. Lorig. 1992. Perceived Self-Efficacy in Self-Management of Chronic Disease. In *Self-Efficacy: Thought Control of Action*. Edited by R. Schwarzer. New York: Hemisphere Publications.

Hover, J., and M. Zimmer. 1978. Nursing Quality Assurance: The Wisconsin System. *Nursing Outlook* 26: 242–248.

Jamieson, M. 1990. Block Nursing: Practicing Autonomous Professional Nursing in the Community. *Nursing and Health Care* 11: 250–263.

Joint Commission on Accreditation of Healthcare Organizations. 1987. The Agenda for Change. Update 1, No. 1: 1–4.

Joint Commission on Accreditation of Hospitals. 1975. *PEP Workbook for Nurses*. Chicago: Joint Commission on Accreditation of Hospitals.

Joos, I., N. Whitman, M. Smith, and R. Nelson. 1992. Nursing Informatics. In *Computers in Small Bytes: The Computer Workbook*. New York: National League for Nursing Press, Publication No. 14-2496.

Kalisch, P. A., and B. J. Kalisch. 1980. Perspectives on Improving Nursing's Public Image. *Nursing and Health Care* 1: 10. Publication No. NCHSR-R-3092. Santa Monica, Calif.

Kelly, K. C., D. G. Huber, M. Johnson, J. C. McCloskey, and M. Maas. 1994. The Medical Outcomes Study: A Nursing Perspective. *Journal of Professional Nursing* 10: 209–216.

Kongstvedt, P. 1995. *Essentials of Managed Care*. Gaithersburg, Md.: Aspen Publishers, Inc.

Kraus, V. L. 1994. *The Effect of Nursing Interventions: Taxonomy of Nursing-Sensitive Patient Outcomes: The Iowa Project*. Proceedings of The Clinical Nurse Specialist Conference, Indianapolis, Ind., October 13–15.

Lamb, G. 1995. Early Lessons Learned from a Capitated Community-Based Nursing Model. *Nursing Administration Quarterly* 19: 18–26.

Lamb, G., N. Donaldson, and J. Kellogg. 1997. *Measuring the Value of Clinical Case Management Programs: A Self-Learning Guide*. Newport Beach, Calif.: Donaldson & Associates.

Landry, C., and J. Knox. 1996. Managed Care Fundamentals: Implications for Health Care Organizations and Health Care Professionals. *American Journal of Occupational Therapy* 50: 413–416.

Larson, C., and F. LaFasto. 1989. *Teamwork: What Must Go Right/What Can Go Wrong*. Newbury Park, Calif.: Sage Publications, Inc.

Leath, C., and R. Thatcher. 1991. Team-Managed Care for Older Adults: A Clinical Demonstration of a Community Model. *Journal of Gerontological Nursing* 17(1): 25–28.

Lefkowich, W. K. 1985. New York State Quality Assurance: An Outcome Oriented System. *American Health Care Association* 11(4): 21–24.

Lewis, B. 1995. HMO Outcomes Research: Lessons From the Field. *Journal of Ambulatory Care Management* 18: 47–55.

Lohr, K. H. 1988. Outcome Measurement: Concepts and Questions. *Inquiry* 25(1): 37–50.

Lohr, K., and R. Brook. 1984. Quality Assurance in Medicine. *American Behavioral Science* 27: 583–607.

Luft, H. 1981. *Health Maintenance Organizations: Dimensions of Performance*. New York: John Wiley.

MacLeod, G. 1995. An Overview of Managed Care. In *Essentials of Managed Health Care*. Edited by P. Kongstvedt. Gaithersburg, Md.: Aspen Publishers, Inc.

Manning, W., J. Newhouse, N. Duan, E. Deller, A. Leibowitz, and S. Marquis. 1987. Health Insurance and the Demand for Medical Care. *American Economic Review* 77: 251–277.

Marek, K. 1989. Outcome Measures in Nursing. *Journal of Nursing Quality Assurance* 4(1):1–9.

Martin, K., G. Leak, and C. Aden. 1992. The Omaha System: A Research-Based Model for Decision-Making. *Journal of Nursing Administration* 22: 47–52.

Martin, K., and N. Scheet. 1992. *The Omaha System: Applications for Community Health Nursing.* Philadelphia, Pa.: W.B. Saunders.

Martin, K., N. Scheet, and M. Stegman. 1993. Home Health Clients, Characteristics, Outcomes of Care, and Nursing Interventions. *Journal of Public Health* 83: 1730–1734.

May, C., C. Schraeder, and T. Britt. 1997. *Managed Care and Case Management: Roles for Professional Nursing.* Washington, D.C.: American Nurses Association.

McCloskey, J. C., and G. M. Bulechek. 1992. Iowa Intervention Project. In *Nursing Interventions Classification (NIC).* Edited by J. C. McClosky and G. M. Bulechek. St. Louis: Mosby–Yearbook.

Miles, K. 1997. Managing Quality from the Utilization Perspective: The Provider View. *Seminars for Nurse Managers* 5: 144–148.

Miller, M., and D. Babcock. 1996. *Critical Thinking Applied to Nursing.* New York: Mosby.

Mundinger, M. 1994. Advanced Practice Nursing: Good Medicine for Physicians? *New England Journal of Medicine* 330: 211–214.

National Center for Nursing Research. 1993. *Nursing Informatics: Enhancing Patient Care.* A report of the NCNR Priority Expert Panel on Nursing Informatics. Bethesda, Md.: U.S. Department of Health and Human Services.

National Institute on Community-Based Long-Term Care. 1990. *Care Management Standards: Guidelines for Practice.* Washington, D.C.: The National Council on the Aging, Inc.

Nightingale, F. 1858. Notes on Matters Affecting the Health, Efficiency, and Hospital Administration of the British Army. London: Harrision and Sons.

O'Connor, P., W. Rush, and N. Pronk. 1997. Database System to Identify Biological Risk in Managed Care Organizations: Implications for Clinical Care. *Journal of Ambulatory Care Management* 20: 17–23.

Ortmeier, B. 1997. Conducting Clinical and Health Economic Outcome Studies in an Ambulatory Setting. *Journal of Ambulatory Care Management* 20: 10–16.

Parr, M. 1996. The Changing Role of Advanced Practice Nursing in a Managed Care Environment. *AACN Clinical Issues* 7 (2): 300–398.

Pew Health Professions Commission. 1995. *Critical Challenges: Revitalizing the Health Professions for the Twenty-first Century.* Executive Summary. Pew Health Professions Commission.

Prospective Payment Assessment Commission. 1997. Medicare and American Health Care System: Report to Congress. Washington, D.C.: Prospective Payment Assessment Commission.

Radosevich, D. 1997. A Framework for Selecting Outcome Measures for Ambulatory Care Research. *Journal of Ambulatory Care Management* 20: 1–9.

Raffel, M., and N. Raffel. 1994. *The U.S. Health System: Origins and Functions,* 4th edition. Albany, N.Y.: Delmar Publishers, Inc.

Rinke, L. 1988. *Outcome Measures in Homecare,* Vol. 3. State of the Art. New York: National League for Nursing.

Roper, W., W. Winkenwerder, G. Hacbarth, and H. Krakauer. 1988. Effectiveness in Health Care: An Initiative to Improve Medical Practice. *New England Journal of Medicine* 319: 1197–1202.

Rustia, J., and J. Bartek. 1997. Managed Care Credentialing of Advanced Practice Nurses. *Nurse Practitioner* 22(9): 90–92, 99–100, 102–103.

Ryan, P., and C. Delaney. 1995. The Nursing Minimum Data Set: Research Findings and Future Directions. In *Annual Review of Nursing Research,* Vol. 13. New York: Springer Publishing.

Scheffler, R., N. Waitzman, and J. Hillman. 1996. The Productivity of Physician Assistants and Nurse Practitioners and Health Work Force Policy in the Era of Managed Health Care. *Journal of Allied Health* 25(3): 207–217.

Schraeder, C., T. Britt, and P. Shelton. 1995. Creating Collaborative Processes in Primary Care. *Primary Practice News* 2(4): 3–5.

Schraeder, C., P. Shelton, T. Britt, D. Dworak, C. Fraser, and J. Grimes. 1997. *Geriatric Collaborative Care Model: Improving the System of Primary Care.* Englewood, Colo.: Center for Research in Ambulatory Health Care Administration.

Schraeder, C., P. Shelton, T. Britt, R. Parker, and J. Leonard. 1997. Population-Based Research Data as a Means to Address Health Outcomes. *Journal of Ambulatory Care Management* 20: 39–46.

Schraeder, C., G. Lamb, P. Shelton, and T. Britt. 1997. Forging a New Nursing Frontier: The Community Nursing Organization. *American Journal of Nursing* 97(1): 63–65.

Shamansky, S. L. 1996. Population-Based Managed Care to Improve Outcomes. *Nursing Economics* 14: 245–247.

Shelton, P., C. Schraeder, D. Dworak, T. Britt, M. Sager, and R. Scully. In press. Geriatric Collaborative Practice as Population-Based Care Strategies. In *1999 Guide to Managed Care Strategies: An Annual Report on the Latest Practices and Policies in the New Managed Care Environment.* Edited by J. Burns and L. Northup. New York: Faulker & Gray.

Shelton, P., C. Schraeder, T. Britt, and R. Kirby. 1994. A Generalist Physician-Based Model for a Rural Geriatric

Collaborative Practice. *Journal of Case Management* 3: 98–104.

Simpson, R. 1997. Take Advantage of Managed Care Opportunities. *Nursing Management* 28(3): 24–25.

Simpson, R. 1994. Nursing Informatics Core Competencies. *Nursing Management* 25: 18, 20.

Simpson, R. 1993. Shifting Perceptions: Defining Nursing Informatics as a Clinical Specialty. *Nursing Management* 24: 20–21.

Simpson, R. 1992. The New Careers in Nursing Informatics. *Nursing Management* 23: 26–27.

Spitzer-Lehmann, R. 1996. "A New Framework for Managed Care: Marrying Finance and Service Delivery." Presented at Managed Care: How to Negotiate and Administer Capitated Contracts, Nursing Management Congress, Chicago, Ill., September 28.

Sprenger, G. 1995. "Healthier Communities: A Paradox in a Capitated Environment." Presented at The Healthcare Quest: Creativity in Capitation, Minneapolis, Minn., July 15–16.

Stahl, D. 1996. Capitation, Point of Service and Medicare Select: Friends or Foes? *Nursing Management* 27(12): 15–18.

Starr, P. 1982. *The Social Transformation of American Medicine.* New York: Basic Books.

Stetler, C. 1987. The Case Manager's Role: A Preliminary Evaluation. *Definition* 2: 1–4.

Tarlov, A. R., J. E. Ware, S. Greenfield, E. C. Nelson, E. Perrin, and M. Zubkoff. 1989. The Medical Outcomes Study: An Application of Methods for Monitoring the Results of Medical Care. *Journal of the American Medical Association* 262: 925–930.

Thorpe, K. 1995. "Health Care Cost Containment: Reflections and Future Directions." In *Health Care Delivery in the United States.* Edited by A. Kovner. New York: Springer Publishing Company.

U.S. Department of Health and Human Services. 1993. *Health Personnel in the United States: Ninth Report to Congress,* 1993: Executive Summary. Washington, D.C.: U.S. Government Printing Office.

Wagner, E. 1996. The Promise and Performance of HMOs in Improving Outcomes in Older Adults. *Journal of the American Geriatrics Society* 44: 1251–1257.

Weil, M., and Karls, J. 1985. Historical Origins and Recent Developments. In *Case Management in Human Service Practice.* Edited by M. Weil and J. Karls. San Francisco: Jossey–Bass.

Weiss, M. 1997. The Quality Evolution in Managed Care Organizations: Shifting the Focus to Community Health. *Journal of Nursing Care Quality* 11(4): 27–31.

Wennberg, J. 1984. Dealing with Medical Practice Variations: A Proposal for Action. *Health Affairs* 3: 6–32.

Werley, H., E. Devine, and C. Zorn. 1988. Nursing Needs its Own Minimum Data Set. *American Journal of Nursing* 88: 1651–1653.

Werley, H., E. Devine, C. Zorn, P. Ryan, and B. Westra. 1991. The Nursing Minimum Data Set: Abstraction Tool for Standardized, Comparable, Essential Data. *American Journal of Public Health* 81(14): 421–426.

Werley, H. H., and N. M. Lang. 1988. The Consensually Derived Nursing Minimum Data Set: Elements and Definitions. In *Identification of the Nursing Minimum Data Set.* Edited by H. H. Werley and N. M. Lang. New York: Springer–Verlag.

Williams, S., and P. Torrens. 1993. *Introduction to Health Services.* Albany, N.Y.: Delmar Publishers.

Wright, R. A. 1993. Community-Oriented Primary Care: The Cornerstone of Health Care Reform. *Journal of the American Medical Association* 269: 2544–2547.

Zielstorff, R., C. Hudgings, S. Grobe, and National Commission on Nursing Implementation Project Task Force on Nursing Information Systems. 1993. *Next Generation Nursing Information Systems: Essential Characteristics for Professional Practice.* Washington, D.C.: American Nurses Association.

Selected Bibliography on Nursing Roles

Applebaum, R., and C. Austin. 1990. *Long Term Care Case Management: Design and Evaluation.* New York: Springer.

Blancett, S., and D. Flarey. 1996. *Case Studies in Nursing Case Management: Health Care Delivery in a World of Managed Care.* Gaithersburg, Md.: Aspen Publishers, Inc.

Bogdonoff, M., S. Hughes, W. Weissert, and E. Paulsen. 1991. *The Living-At-Home Program: Innovations in Service Access and Case Management.* New York: Springer Publishing Company.

Del Tongo-Armanasco, V., A. Hopkin, and S. Harter. 1993. *Collaborative Nursing Case Management: A Handbook for Development and Implementation.* New York: Springer Publishing Company.

Etherege, M.1989. *Collaborative Care: Nursing Case Management.* Chicago, Ill.: American Hospital Publishing, Inc.

Flarey, D., and S. Blancett. 1996. *Handbook of Nursing Case Management: Health Care Delivery in a World of Managed Care.* Gaithersburg, Md.: Aspen Publishers, Inc.

Mullahy, C. 1995. *The Case Manager's Handbook.* Gaithersburg, Md.: Aspen Publishers, Inc.

Newell, M. 1996. *Using Nursing Case Management to Improve Health Outcomes.* Gaithersburg, Md.: Aspen Publishers, Inc.

Schraeder, C., P. Shelton, T. Britt, and K. Buttitta. 1996. Case Management in a Capitated System: The Community Nursing Organization. *Journal of Case Management* 5: 58–64.

Zerwekh, J., and J. Claborn. 1997. *Nursing Today: Transition and Trends.* Philadelphia, Pa.: W.B. Saunders Company.